HARNESSING
AI & DATA SCIENCE
FOR REAL WORLD IMPACT

Tosin Clement

TABLE OF CONTENTS

PREFACE

This book was born from a question I kept hearing over and over again: "What does real-world data science actually look like in action?" It is a question that sits at the intersection of promise and pressure, of innovation and integrity. As the field of AI and data science rapidly evolves, practitioners need not only technical guidance but a model of applied excellence they can learn from.

My journey is not just a series of projects and titles; it's a masterclass in deploying intelligence where it counts. From deploying machine learning models in enterprise environments to championing ethical frameworks in data use, I have helped redefine the modern role of the data scientist. This book offers more than technical blueprints. It offers reflections, narratives, and frameworks that show how one can integrate innovation with responsibility, impact with integrity.

Whether you are a seasoned professional or a student stepping into the data world for the first time, I hope this book helps you bridge theory with impact, and ambition with discipline.

INTRODUCTION

We are living in an era defined by data. From personalized financial services to global healthcare diagnostics, AI and data science are the engines behind decisions both grand and granular. But for all the buzzwords and breakthroughs, there is still a critical need for voices that illustrate how data science works not just in theory, but in practice. This book chronicles my applied journey as a data scientist whose career offers lessons in precision, purpose, and progress.

In the following chapters, we explore foundational principles of secure data analysis, the design and deployment of machine learning models, and how real-world use cases from fraud detection to anomaly monitoring, come alive through thoughtful engineering. We also dive into the complexities of mentoring new data scientists, initiating organizational innovation, and contributing to the field through impactful research.

Ultimately, this is not just a story. It is a framework for every reader who seeks to do meaningful work at the crossroads of data and responsibility. Let's begin.

CHAPTER 1

I did not stumble into data science by accident. My path was not paved with trends or fast-track certifications, but with a deliberate commitment to understanding how information shapes decisions, and how systems whether social, economic, or digital can be understood through structured inquiry. Before machine learning, before model training, and long before the term 'AI' became mainstream in business meetings, I was asking questions rooted in curiosity: Why do systems behave the way they do? What hidden variables shape outcomes? And how can we learn from patterns that aren't immediately visible?

Those questions would later define my signature approach, but his journey began with what many might consider unglamorous, statistical theory, data cleaning, and the discipline of structuring raw data into insight-ready formats. Long before my career took off, I spent hours confronting datasets that didn't make sense at first glance. There were inconsistencies to resolve, missing values to address, and frameworks to design. But rather than seeing this work as mundane, I saw it as foundational. It was in these early days that he began to understand a truth that would guide his entire career: data science is less about algorithms and more about clarity.

Clarity, for I, meant translating complexity into understanding. It meant knowing not just how to run a regression model, but why that model was appropriate for the problem at hand. It meant questioning assumptions, checking bias, and making sure that any insight generated could be trusted in the real world. These instincts were sharpened not only in classrooms and code editors, but also through his early internships and entry-level roles, spaces where mistakes were learning moments and rigor was non-negotiable.

My formal education gave me theoretical tools: linear algebra, probability, statistical inference, data structures, and programming in languages like Python and R. But it was his habit of reflection that made these tools come alive. I didn't just learn formulas; he sought to understand how they behaved across contexts. When he encountered errors, he didn't stop fixing them, I explored why they occurred and how they might be prevented. This pattern of reflective practice would come to define my reputation as someone whose knowledge ran deeper than the syntax.

One pivotal moment came when I worked on a university project involving crime data and public safety interventions. The data was fragmented and poorly documented, collected from multiple agencies with no central standard. Many would have seen the task as thankless. I saw it as an opportunity to create order out of chaos. Over several months, I and my team developed a method for harmonizing and analyzing the data to uncover patterns in response times and incident frequencies. The result was more than just a good grade; it was a recognition that thoughtful data analysis could drive better outcomes for public systems.

This experience solidified a core belief that would later define his work in professional environments: good data science doesn't start with algorithms; it starts with questions. And even before the questions, it starts with mindset. A mindset that values exploration over shortcuts, depth over decoration, and learning over ego.

As my career began to take shape, I remained committed to this foundation. Whether working on small prototypes or enterprise-level analytics systems, I approached every project with the same foundational rigor. I listened first. I clarified objectives. I defined success metrics. I ensured data quality before writing a single line of modeling code. These habits developed early, became part of my identity as a data scientist.

In the years to come, I would go on to lead high-impact projects and mentor young professionals. But the roots of impact lay in these foundational habits of thinking clearly, questioning deeply, and building with integrity. In one notable example, I was asked to optimize user engagement across a client's digital product suite. The data was massive, distributed, and messy. But I didn't rush into building predictive models. I started by questioning the existing KPIs. Were they measuring the right things? Were there hidden user behaviors that weren't being tracked? I spent weeks cleaning logs, validating assumptions, and building exploration visualizations before suggesting a single algorithm. This careful diligence revealed that one of the most celebrated product features was actually driving drop-offs. It wasn't a model that saved the business money, it was insight.

This episode became one of the defining moments in my development. It reinforced a belief I had nurtured since my university days: the most valuable data scientists are not those who know the most tools, but those who know how to ask the right questions. From that point onward, I made it a personal rule to never present a model or dashboard without framing it in terms of the question it was designed to answer and the assumptions it relied on. This principle became especially critical when he later began working with C-level executives who didn't want technical jargon, they wanted clarity.

As I moved into more senior roles, I became a bridge between disciplines. He was the person who could translate business objectives into data workflows and vice versa. He wasn't just a data scientist anymore; he had become an integrator and a rare figure who could navigate meetings with engineers, analysts, product managers, and legal teams with equal ease. The communication skills were not accidental. From early on, I had trained myself not just to write clean code but to write clear documentation and tell compelling stories with data. I believed that analysis that couldn't be understood by stakeholders was no better than noise.

Over time, this clarity of thought and communication became his signature. When new employees joined the team, it was I who mentored them on how to frame problems, how to document their workflows, and how to anticipate questions in their presentations. My goal was never to build dependency, but to foster independence.

In parallel with this technical growth, I also developed a keen interest in organizational behavior. I read widely on topics ranging from decision science to behavioral economics and systems theory. I began to see data science not just as a technical field but as a human one. Behind every dataset were real people, customers, users, citizens whose lives were shaped by the algorithms and insights produced. This awareness added a layer of humility to his work. It reminded me that every outlier had a story, and every metric had a margin of error. It deepened my appreciation for the responsibility that came with his craft.

Looking back, my early journey into data science reveals a profound truth: excellence in this field is not built in bursts of brilliance but in the quiet, sustained discipline of inquiry, ethics, and execution. From wrangling chaotic spreadsheets to building enterprise systems, every step in his story underscores the value of a data-driven mindset, one that prizes clarity, curiosity, and consequence over trends, tools, or titles.

CHAPTER 2

Trust is not technically deliverable. It is not built with lines of code, and it cannot be guaranteed by compliance checklists. In data science, trust must be engineered deliberately, baked into every decision, every model, and every assumption. I learned this lesson early and it would go on to shape every ethical stance, framework, and innovation he became known for. In an industry driven by efficiency and novelty, he emerged as a practitioner who never lost sight of the responsibility attached to each data point.

Ethics in data science is often misunderstood as a reactive discipline, something to be applied once damage has been done or when public scrutiny forces a policy change. I challenged this notion by building ethics into the architecture of every project from the very beginning. For me, ethics was not an add-on; it was an engineering principle.

The origin of this perspective traces back to a time when I was involved in designing a customer behavior model for a digital lending platform. The model worked too well, in fact. It identified high-risk borrowers with incredible accuracy, allowing the business to avoid potential losses. But it also surfaced a troubling trend: the model disproportionately flagged applicants from specific low-income regions. On paper, this was statistically valid. In practice, it raised deep concerns about fairness, access, and algorithmic discrimination.

While many on the team were content with the model's performance, I raised the red flag. I led a conversation initially uncomfortable about model bias, training data, and the socio-economic factors embedded invisibly within the data pipeline. I didn't just point out the problem; I built a new version of the model that accounted for structural inequities, introducing a correction factor that preserved accuracy while dramatically improving fairness. The outcome was a more inclusive lending strategy that didn't penalize applicants for systemic disadvantages beyond their control.

This moment marked a pivot. I began advocating for model interpretability, transparent pipelines, and ethical review boards within data-driven companies. I joined forums that worked on setting ethical standards for predictive analytics and actively contributed to papers on bias mitigation and risk-sensitive modeling. For me, the goal wasn't perfection, it was accountability.

I often argue that ethical lapses in data science are rarely born of malice. More often, they are the result of abstraction: when data scientists work too far removed from the people their models affect. I challenged his peers to collapse that distance to see the faces behind the features, the households behind the histograms. Through workshops, keynotes, and mentorship, he helped others move beyond mere performance metrics and embrace a more holistic understanding of model impact.

One of the most powerful frameworks I introduced in teams was what I called "ethics pre-mortems." Before launching any model, the team would brainstorm potential negative externalities not just technical failures, but unintended human consequences. They asked: Who could be harmed by this model? What assumptions might backfire? What biases might be reinforced? This exercise didn't slow projects down as it accelerated insight. It led to better models, not just safer ones.

Ethical engineering also meant knowing when not to model. In one memorable instance, I was brought in to advise on a facial recognition prototype meant for access control at a corporate facility. The model had high accuracy in testing, but I noted its skewed false rejection rates for employees with darker skin tones, a common flaw in many commercial facial recognition systems. Rather than fine-tuning the model in isolation, he raised a more fundamental question: Should facial recognition be used at all for this purpose? The organization eventually pivoted itself to a secure but more inclusive biometric alternative, prioritizing usability and fairness.

This episode underscored a recurring theme in my philosophy: not everything that can be modeled should be modeled. Just because a solution is technically feasible doesn't make it ethically sound. My decisions were often guided by a three-part principle he shared widely: clarity, consent, and consequence. Clarity in how the model works, consent from those impacted, and consequence analysis to explore ripple effects.

My commitment to data ethics also extended into education. I developed internal workshops for new data scientists focused not just on algorithms, but on values. These sessions involved roleplay scenarios, bias detection challenges, and real-world case studies drawn from experiences. The goal was simple: make ethics tangible. Over time, my voice became respected in wider circles. I was invited to contribute to cross-industry panels on responsible AI, helped co-author policy recommendations for government agencies, and was recognized for pushing for algorithmic accountability in environments where profit pressures often eclipsed ethical deliberation.

Despite all this, I never portrayed myself as an ethics savior. I acknowledged the complexity, the compromises, and the gray areas. I admitted when I got things wrong. In my view, ethical integrity wasn't about having all the answers but about asking the right questions and creating space for them in the rush to innovate.

By integrating ethics into design, I helped redefine what it means to be a data scientist. Showing that the trust users place in data systems is earned not through slogans, but through the deliberate architecture of fairness, transparency, and accountability.

The focus on the ethical application of data science didn't remain confined to boardrooms or strategy decks, it found its way into some of the most high-stakes projects across different sectors, including public health, financial inclusion, and education reform. My belief that ethical oversight must be active, not passive, became especially critical when I led a collaborative initiative with a regional health ministry seeking to deploy predictive models for resource allocation during a disease outbreak.

The project aimed to anticipate spikes in infection rates across underserved areas. Data was pulled from hospital records, mobility tracking, and social media sentiment, sources that were rich in insight but also laden with privacy concerns. I immediately implemented a multi-stage data anonymization pipeline and set clear data access protocols for every stakeholder. While the urgency of the crisis tempted many to cut corners in favor of faster deployment, I insisted on ethical discipline. The final model helped allocate medical resources more efficiently, but it also preserved patient dignity and community trust. It was a victory not just in predictive accuracy, but in principled design.

In another high-impact engagement, I worked on a partnership between a financial institution and a government agency aimed at increasing credit access for women-owned businesses in rural communities. The original approach was to use mobile transaction history and telco metadata to generate creditworthiness scores. I noticed early on that the dataset underrepresented women due to shared mobile usage and informal lending practices that left little digital trace. Instead of pushing forward with a flawed dataset, he proposed the integration of qualitative inputs like local cooperative participation and repayment trust ratings collected via SMS surveys. The hybrid scoring system became a pilot model for inclusive fintech innovation and helped rewrite assumptions about what constituted reliable financial data.

These examples illuminate a fundamental trait in my professional philosophy: ethics is not a brake on innovation, rather it is its catalyst. When properly embedded, ethical design unlocks new possibilities, stronger adoption, and deeper user loyalty. This belief challenged the common industry misconception that ethical oversight slows down product cycles. In my experience, ethical missteps were far costlier both financially and reputationally than building trust from the beginning.

As my career progressed, I began advocating not just for ethical data science practices, but for ethical leadership. I mentored startup founders, consulted with regulatory bodies, and trained corporate leaders on how to integrate ethical questions into every stage of digital product development. I developed a toolkit he called "The Ethical Check-In," a set of ten reflective prompts used by teams at major project milestones. These included questions like: Who benefits from this system? Who might be excluded? If this product fails, who gets hurt? Are there data gaps we are ignoring due to convenience?

This proactive approach to trust-building became part of the legacy. It wasn't just about avoiding harm; it was about earning legitimacy in the eyes of users and stakeholders. My reputation for balancing innovation with integrity led to invitations to consult internationally, where he helped design ethical frameworks for AI governance programs and advised on the safe adoption of predictive models in sectors ranging from agriculture to law enforcement.

Perhaps most notably, my work began influencing public discourse. I was featured in think tank reports, quoted in policy papers, and frequently asked to speak on national platforms. Yet he remained grounded in practice. For every panel appearance, there were hours spent helping junior data scientists troubleshoot ethical dilemmas on internal Slack channels. For every white paper, there were grassroots efforts to open access to data ethics education in underserved communities.

One of my contributions in this chapter of my journey was a community-led initiative aimed at teaching ethical data science to secondary school students. The curriculum was simplified but never condescending. Students learned about privacy by analyzing their digital footprints, explored bias through games that demonstrated how algorithms could reinforce stereotypes, and discussed fairness through debates around real-world technologies like facial recognition and targeted advertising. It was my way of scaling ethical intuition planting seeds that could grow into responsible practice decades ahead.

In retrospect, my influence on ethical data science is not measured by the number of talks he gave or the companies he advised. It is measured by the shift in mindset he inspired. By embedding trust into the very structure of data systems long before it became trendy or mandated, he set a precedent. He showed that building ethical systems is not about heroics; it is about habits. Not about saying the right things after a breach but doing the right things before one happens.

The second half of this chapter affirms what the first half established: that trust is engineered, not inherited. Through real-world interventions, inclusive design, and public education, I have shown that the most powerful models we can build are not just intelligent, they are just. And in a future increasingly defined by automation and abstraction, that kind of trust might be our most vital form of intelligence.

CHAPTER 3

The journey from a working model on a laptop to an intelligent system embedded in a real-world application is a canyon few projects cross successfully. Within the sterile confines of notebooks and sandbox environments, a machine learning model may achieve stunning accuracy, elegant performance curves, and predictive finesse. But the real world is not static. It is not clean. It is rarely well-documented. And it is certainly not organized to accommodate idealized algorithms.

Many projects fail not because the ideas are flawed, but because the environments they are built for are more chaotic and dynamic than anticipated. The moment a model leaves development and faces live users, its limitations surface, data pipelines break under unpredictable loads, inference lags spike under peak traffic, and small changes in upstream systems lead to compounding errors. The bridge from theory to practice is built on system thinking, architectural resilience, and a deep respect for operational reality.

This subsection examines the difficult transition from model development to system deployment. It investigates how teams move from theoretical performance to production-grade reliability. In the ecosystem of intelligent systems, success isn't defined by precision alone, it is defined by whether that precision can be sustained at scale, over time, under pressure.

In the early days of enterprise data science, the deployment of a machine learning model was often treated as an afterthought. Teams focused on notebooks, exploratory data analysis, and cross-validation scores, with deployment deferred to "the devs" downstream. This separation created a bottleneck. Models were rarely production-ready because they were never designed to be. They lacked considerations for runtime performance, monitoring, versioning, or retraining schedules. As a result, models that worked in isolated conditions failed once embedded in operational systems.

This pattern began to shift with the rise of MLOps which was a discipline that integrates machine learning development with DevOps principles. In mature teams, deployment is not a phase, it is part of design. The earliest planning documents consider how the model will be served, how it will access data in real time, how it will scale, and how it will recover from failure. Infrastructure is no longer an afterthought. It is part of intelligence.

Take, for instance, the development of a customer support classifier for a financial institution. In a prototype environment, the model may perform well on historic emails, correctly categorizing 92% of queries into predefined classes. However, in production, the system is expected to handle real-time chat streams, respond within milliseconds, and adapt to new categories that emerge from product changes or customer behavior. The underlying infrastructure must support streaming data ingestion, low-latency inference, and continuous learning pipelines. If these are not built into the original architecture, the model's practical value will deteriorate quickly, regardless of its offline metrics.

The transition from prototype to production often reveals a key truth: intelligent systems are not just about models; they are about ecosystems. A good model inside a brittle system is still a brittle solution. This understanding compels architects to think holistically. They build feedback loops, failover systems, and fallback strategies. They instrument everything because what cannot be observed cannot be trusted. Logging, alerting, and metrics dashboards are not optional tools; they are safeguards against the entropy of live environments.

One common failure point in real-world deployment is data drift. Models trained on yesterday's data often falter when the world changes. For example, a fraud detection system trained on patterns from 2020 might underperform in 2023, where new tactics and user behaviors dominate. In sandbox tests, this drift is invisible. In production, it becomes a liability. Production-grade systems must include mechanisms for detecting drift, triggering retraining, or even self-updating. It is no longer acceptable to "set and forget." Intelligent systems must be designed to learn continuously or at the very least, be monitored continuously for signs of decay.

Latency is another silent killer. In academic settings, few papers optimize for runtime speed. But in production, latency is often the determining factor in user satisfaction. A recommendation engine that delivers the perfect suggestion after five seconds is far less valuable than one that delivers a good enough suggestion in 200 milliseconds. System builders must learn to optimize not just for accuracy, but for experience. They must balance model complexity with inference speed, precision with cost, and innovation with usability.

Building intelligent systems also means accounting for failures not as exceptions, but as inevitabilities. Networks fail. APIs timeout. Input formats change. Good systems are not those that avoid failure; they are those that handle it gracefully. This demands defensive programming, redundancy in critical paths, and circuit-breaker mechanisms that ensure system stability even when individual components misbehave.

One illustrative example comes from the development of a supply chain optimization tool used by a regional logistics firm. Initially trained on historic delivery data, the model accurately predicted late shipments based on weather, traffic, and warehouse load. But when it was deployed, it crashed within hours. The reason? The data pipeline feeding real-time weather updates relied on an external API that rate-limited requests after a threshold. The prototype had never simulated load conditions. Once in production, the system made too many requests and was blocked. The fix was not a better model, it was a better architecture: caching strategies, rate-limiting policies, and graceful fallbacks.

These lessons become embedded not in theory, but in scars. Teams who have lived through production incidents build systems differently. They anticipate failure. They design for chaos. They treat deployment not as a finish line but as the beginning of a new lifecycle and one that demands continuous testing, automated rollback strategies, and human-in-the-loop checks for high-stakes decisions.

There is also a cultural shift required. Teams that excel in production deployments foster habits that go beyond code. They write documentation that anticipates future readers. They share learnings from incidents transparently. They design onboarding materials for the next engineer who will inherit the system. In short, they build with continuity in mind.

At its core, the move from prototype to production is not about polishing a model, it is about changing how teams think about intelligence. Intelligence that cannot operate reliably in the real world is not truly intelligent. By embedding infrastructure into the very definition of success, organizations can build systems that are not just accurate in theory, but resilient, scalable, and valuable in practice.

This is the frontier of real-world data science does not model that impress in isolation, but systems that endure in complexity. And in this space, engineering discipline is as valuable as algorithmic innovation. The canyon between idea and impact can be crossed but only by those willing to build bridges that last.

Intelligent systems are only as powerful as the pipelines that feed them. Underneath every high-performing machine learning model is a living network of components that transform raw data into usable insight, often in real time, and often under conditions far messier than the tidy world of research environments. This subsection dives into the heart of those operations, the unseen machinery that transforms potential into production.

To build a pipeline that works in the real world is to embrace complexity, manage uncertainty, and design for iteration. It begins with data acquisition. Unlike classroom datasets with clearly defined boundaries, production data is fragmented, unstructured, and often arrives in bursts. Whether it's transactional records from millions of users, sensor readings from distributed IoT devices, or clickstreams from web platforms, the pipeline must begin by ingesting data in its natural, untamed form. This task alone can overwhelm teams who focus too narrowly on model selection rather than the infrastructure necessary to feed it.

A robust pipeline doesn't treat raw data as a nuisance, rather it treats it as a first-class citizen. Data validation becomes a foundational step, not an afterthought. Pipelines are built to inspect, clean, and normalize inputs on the fly. They reject malformed records, fill missing values according to statistical logic, and tag anomalies for downstream inspection. These early steps are where the system defends itself from decay. When overlooked, they become the source of costly failures downstream.

Next comes feature engineering, the subtle art of translating raw inputs into meaningful signals. This is where domain knowledge meets algorithmic intuition. In traditional workflows, this stage might happen manually, offline, and inconsistently across environments. But in production systems, feature engineering must be automated, repeatable, and version controlled. Every transformation whether a rolling average, a one-hot encoding, or a learned embedding must be reproducible from logs and traceable back to source. Otherwise, explanations break, audit trails vanish, and trust erodes.

Batch pipelines often perform these tasks overnight, processing daily transaction logs and producing fresh features before the morning's predictions. But real-time systems demand stream processing, event-driven pipelines that update models continuously as new data arrives. Here, tools like Apache Kafka, Spark Streaming, and Flink orchestrate flows that operate within milliseconds. These are the beating hearts of real-world AI, pushing data through the veins of distributed architectures to ensure the model always sees the latest version of reality.

With features in place, the system turns into inference. A model is only useful if it can produce predictions when they're needed, not hours later. Serving architectures vary from RESTful microservices to embedded edge inference systems. But they share a goal: low-latency, high-availability responses that integrate seamlessly with other components. To achieve this, models must be serialized into efficient formats, served behind scalable APIs, and containerized for consistent deployment. This is not where the data scientist's job ends, it is where it expands into software engineering.

But inference is not the end. Downstream from predictions lie decision engines, business logic, and action systems. A fraud prediction means little unless it triggers a transaction block. A demand forecast is useless unless it adjusts inventory thresholds. Intelligent systems do not stop at insight as they act. Pipelines must be wired to downstream systems that consume predictions and drive business outcomes. This is where collaboration between data teams and operations teams becomes essential.

Monitoring sits quietly beside every stage of the pipeline. Good systems observe not only outputs but also inputs, transformation steps, model behavior, and system health. Monitoring dashboards track prediction volumes, distribution drifts, and system errors. Alerts are calibrated not to overreact to noise but to flag real threats, rather spikes in response time, missing features, or memory bottlenecks. Observability is not a bonus feature; it is the only way to ensure that what's working today keeps working tomorrow.

Underneath this entire structure lies a versioning layer, one that tracks models, data, features, and configurations. Reproducibility is the contract every system makes with the future. When a model fails or misbehaves, versioning allows teams to rewind the clock. What data was used? What transformations were applied? What thresholds were set? Without this, debugging becomes guesswork. With it, debugging becomes discipline.

Modern teams increasingly use orchestration tools like Airflow or Dragster to tie these components together. These tools define dependencies, manage schedules, and allow pipelines to scale across compute clusters. But no matter what the tool, the principle remains: pipelines must be clear, resilient, and observable. They must be designed to grow as data grows, evolve as needs evolve, and recover when things go wrong.

The anatomy of the pipeline is not static. It evolves. New data sources emerge. Feature definitions change. Models are retrained. Business priorities shift. A pipeline built without flexibility becomes brittle. A pipeline designed with modularity adapts. Intelligent systems, then, are not just powered by smart models, they are enabled by smart pipelines.

In organizations where these pipelines flourish, there is a shared understanding that infrastructure is not a support function, it is a product. It is versioned, maintained, documented, and tested. It has owners. It has users. And it has a lifecycle. By treating pipelines as first-class systems, teams move from building isolated solutions to building intelligent ecosystems ones that scale, adapt, and deliver real-world impact every day.

At the heart of every intelligent system lies a set of trade-offs, tensions that force teams to prioritize, to compromise, and ultimately, to make decisions that shape the user experience in profound ways. One of the most persistent trade-offs in real-world AI deployment is that between latency and accuracy. The notion that better models are simply more accurate models is a seductive one, but it collapses under the weight of real-time systems, edge computing constraints, and human attention spans.

The pursuit of higher accuracy is deeply ingrained in the culture of data science. In academic benchmarks and Kaggle competitions, leaderboards are dominated by tenths-of-a-percent improvements. But in the field, where milliseconds matter and compute costs scale with usage, the calculus changes. Accuracy, it turns out, is not free. It has a latency cost. A complexity cost. A stability cost. And in many cases, the marginal gain in precision does not justify the operational overhead it incurs.

Consider a product recommendation engine embedded in a high-traffic e-commerce platform. A model that improves the click-through rate by 1.5% might be celebrated in a research paper. But if it takes three seconds longer to generate results compared to a simpler model that achieves 1.2% improvement, the trade-off fails. Users drop off. Pages don't load. Trust erodes. The elegance of the model is invisible to the customer; their experience is shaped entirely by speed and relevance. In these scenarios, good-enough and fast often beats best and slow.

Intelligent system builders understand this. They know that real-world deployment is a game of prioritizing usability over purity. Sometimes, this means compressing models to fit into memory-constrained environments. Sometimes, it means using approximate algorithms that sacrifice some precision for consistent responsiveness. And sometimes, it means walking away from flashy ensemble methods in favor of interpretable models that are easier to debug and maintain.

The cost of cleverness also shows up in system complexity. Complex models often require more elaborate preprocessing, more intricate feature pipelines, and more nuanced tuning. This increases the surface area for failure. More moving parts mean more things that can go wrong. And when systems fail especially in customer-facing applications, it doesn't matter how brilliant the algorithm is if the service is down or unusable.

A particularly illustrative example is the use of deep learning in document classification for legal services. Initial pilots using large transformer-based models achieved impressive F1 scores. But during testing, the inference time per document exceeded acceptable thresholds for real-time analysis. Additionally, infrastructure costs ballooned due to GPU provisioning. The team ultimately switched to a fine-tuned logistic regression model, backed by robust feature engineering. The performance dropped slightly, but latency improved tenfold, and system uptime increased dramatically. Clients noticed the improvement in speed, not the dip in precision.

Another context where latency dominates is fraud detection. In high-frequency transaction environments, such as mobile payments or online banking, models must operate within a few hundred milliseconds. Any delay beyond that triggers fallback systems or manual intervention, disrupting the customer journey. In such cases, the system's responsiveness is the feature, not the model's ROC curve. Engineers here optimize for throughput, stability, and interpretability. The model becomes a component of a larger risk pipeline that includes heuristics, user context, and real-time behavioral rules.

Beyond speed, there's the question of explainability. Complex models often deliver predictions that no one, not even their creators, can easily explain. In industries where decisions must be auditable, such as healthcare or lending, this becomes a barrier to adoption. A black-box model that takes hours to train and seconds to explain is less valuable than a transparent model that can be interrogated in real time. Sometimes the cleverest solution is the one you can stand behind in a meeting with regulators.

This doesn't mean accuracy should be dismissed. It remains vital, especially in high-stakes domains where false positives and negatives have real consequences. But accuracy must be considered within a broader performance envelope. An intelligent system is not a static model; it is a living organism. It interacts with infrastructure, users, edge devices, networks, regulations, and business needs. Each of these imposes constraints that transform accuracy from a destination into a variable, something to be tuned, not idolized.

The best builders do not chase cleverness for their own sake. They chase value. They measure success not in terms of algorithmic novelty but in terms of real-world outcomes. Are users satisfied? Are systems stable? Are engineers able to maintain and evolve the stack? These questions matter far more than the decimal point on a validation set.

Latency, accuracy, and cleverness form a triangle of competing interests. Rarely can all three be maximized at once. Intelligent system design is the art of navigating these constraints gracefully. It is the act of choosing what to sacrifice in order to deliver what matters. And in that act of prioritization, the true craft of engineering begins.

Deploying an intelligent system into the wild means inviting unpredictability. Data arrives late. APIs break. User behavior shifts. And when systems fail because they inevitably will, it is not just functionality that breaks. Trust breaks. Trust is what allows users, stakeholders, and engineers to lean on a system, depend on it, and expect it to behave consistently in the face of change. It is not something that gets tacked on in the final sprint before release. It must be engineered from day one.

A truly intelligent system is not only measured by how smart its algorithms are, but by how gracefully it handles the unexpected. Trust is engineered through layers: through security, through observability, and through redundancy. Each layer acts as a reinforcement, not just for system health but for the relationship between the system and its users.

Security is the first wall. Intelligent systems often operate on sensitive data, financial records, personal health information, and behavioral signals. These datasets are not merely assets; they are liabilities if mishandled. The architecture must prioritize encryption, authentication, and access control. Every pipeline stage from ingestion, transformation, inference, storage must be secured. Secrets must be vaulted. Logs must be scrubbed. And every input must be treated as potentially malicious. Building secure-by-default systems isn't paranoid, it's prudent.

Yet technical security alone does not protect against every failure. That's where observability becomes vital. A system that cannot see itself cannot protect itself. It is not enough to know that something has gone wrong. The system must reveal what, where, and why. Metrics, logs, and traces together form the trinity of modern observability. They must be designed intentionally. Metrics track model performance, system latency, error rates, and data freshness. Logs capture context, what the system was doing and what it saw. Traces follow requests across services, mapping journeys from frontend interaction to backend computation.

In practice, this means integrating tools like Prometheus, Grafana, Open Telemetry, and custom-built dashboards. But it also means building a culture where observability is not viewed as overhead, but as armor. Teams should be able to answer: What happened just before that spike in errors? Which feature pipeline failed? Did model predictions degrade before or after the deployment of the new version?

This continuous introspection is what separates brittle systems from resilient ones. When monitoring systems are passive, failures propagate in silence. But when monitoring systems are active when they notify, visualize, and learn they form a protective layer that detects issues before users do.

Redundancy is the final shield. It is what allows systems to degrade gracefully instead of catastrophically. Redundancy can mean horizontal scaling, where multiple model replicas share the load. It can mean fallback models, simpler algorithms that take over when complex systems go offline. It can mean caching recent predictions or precomputing responses for common inputs. The goal is not to eliminate failure, but to ensure that failure does not compromise the system's core promise to the user.

Consider an automated underwriting engine for digital loans. In normal operation, the system uses a real-time model that analyzes credit history, transaction data, and behavioral signals. But during peak traffic, inference may lag. A redundant path kicks in—rules-based heuristics that handle low-risk applications automatically while queuing complex ones for model-based review. From the user's perspective, the system remains responsive. Internally, it absorbs strain and prevents collapse.

Redundancy also applies to data ingestion. Real-time systems must be designed to handle delayed streams, missing packets, and out-of-order records. Message queues, checkpointing mechanisms, and idempotent processing logic ensure that even under stress, the system does not lose integrity. To engineer trust is to anticipate betrayal. Every component is a candidate for failure. Every API is a handshake that might be dropped. Systems of trust are built by asking, "What happens if these breaks?" and then designing the answer into the architecture. This mindset shifts teams from reactive firefighting to proactive design.

It also influences how teams are structured. Reliable systems are not built by brilliant individuals, but they are maintained by teams that share ownership, rotate responsibilities, and document tribal knowledge. Runbooks are created not for compliance, but for continuity. Chaos engineering exercises are run not for drama, but for confidence. Ultimately, systems of trust are not just technical achievements, they are social contracts. When a user relies on a predictive system to recommend a medication, flag a financial anomaly, or guide a hiring decision, they are placing trust in more than code. They are trusting the process, the people, and the principles behind that system. To honor that trust, the system must be ready not just to succeed, but to fail with dignity.

This is what separates good systems from great ones. Not just the ability to function when conditions are perfect, but the resilience to serve when the world is messy, delayed, or broken. Security, observability, and redundancy form the foundation of this resilience. Together, they create intelligent systems that not only deliver value but deserve the trust they are given.

CHAPTER 4

Intelligent systems don't become impactful just because they work. They become impactful when they work reliably across time, scale, environments, and edge cases. A prototype that performs well in a controlled setting might make headlines, but unless it evolves into a resilient, extensible, and context-aware platform, its influence remains limited. The difference between a clever experiment and a true innovation is often found in what happens next when a working concept is asked to perform on a scale.

Scaling an intelligent system is not merely a technical exercise in adding servers or optimizing code. It is a systemic transformation. What works for a thousand users might crumble under a million. What performs well on a city's dataset might misfire entirely in a rural setting. What succeeds in a single language, regulatory environment, or hardware configuration might break apart when those assumptions no longer hold. Scaling is not simply about making something bigger, it is about making something *stronger* while making it *available*.

This transformation requires a different mindset from the outset. Most early-stage projects are developed with a narrow scope. The team knows the use case. The data is curated. The environment is familiar. But success breeds ambition, and ambition leads to demands for replication. Teams are asked to "take what works and scale it" as though it were a matter of copying and pasting. But the context in which a prototype was born is almost never replicated in new environments.

The first barrier to scale is often fragility. Intelligent systems trained on small, clean datasets under specific operational conditions tend to be fragile when exposed to the noise and diversity of reality. For example, an early AI customer support agent might perform exceptionally well on internal company data, where queries follow known formats and language patterns. But the moment it is exposed to the public, where phrasing varies, edge cases multiply, and abusive language appears, its limitations surface. Scaling, in this context, is not just about handling more queries, it's about handling *different* queries. Robustness, not raw performance, becomes the key metric.

Another challenge emerges in governance. As an intelligent system grows, so too does the need for oversight. In a prototype, errors may be rare, and their impact minimal. But on a scale, those same errors multiply and can affect real users, finances, or reputations. A 2% false positive rate may sound small in a lab but when applied to millions of transactions, it means thousands of incorrect decisions every day. Scaling a system means scaling its responsibility.

This is where platform thinking begins to diverge from prototype thinking. Platforms aren't just tools that solve problems, they are environments that enable continuous use, iteration, and adaptation. A platform is built to last, to be inherited, and to grow. It must be observable, extensible, and operable by people other than its original creators. This shift requires re-architecting the system with modularity, documentation, interfaces, and version control baked into its foundations.

In the transition from pilot to platform, teams also confront the question of ownership. Who maintains the model? Who updates the training data? Who retrains it as a business goals shift, or external variables change? In a prototype, the answers are simple, the original developers. In a platform, ownership is distributed. Documentation becomes more than a courtesy; it becomes a contract. Automation replaces ad hoc procedures. Retraining pipelines must be continuous or scheduled, not manual. And governance bodies, data stewards, ethical reviewers, compliance officers enter the scene to ensure that scale does not outpace accountability.

Consider the case of a regional health analytics model designed to predict hospital admissions during flu season. Initially piloted in one metropolitan area, the system used real-time clinic reports, weather data, and pharmacy sales to forecast resource needs. When it was successful, stakeholders wanted to scale it nationwide. But that required a major redesign. Rural areas had less frequent reporting. Some regions used different healthcare coding systems. Others had privacy restrictions that altered data granularity. Scaling the model meant rewriting parts of it to adapt to new data realities. It meant rethinking features that were highly localized. It also meant introducing safeguards so that model performance could be continuously validated across vastly different contexts.

What this story reveals is that scaling isn't about making the model more powerful, it's about making it more *context aware*. A model that works in isolation must be taught to work in a network. A system that handles single-region logic must evolve to accommodate jurisdictional variation. A prototype that makes assumptions must grow into a platform that tests them.

As platforms mature, they often attract new users with new needs. What began as a tool for operational efficiency might be expected to serve as a strategic insight engine. A model built to predict churn may be asked to power real-time user personalization. With each new use case, complexity compounds. Without a clear architecture, systems become brittle. Without clear priorities, feature creep sets in. And without a plan for scale from the beginning, even brilliant systems risk collapse under their own weight.

One key to sustainable scaling lies in abstraction. Teams must identify which parts of the system should remain constant and which should vary across deployments. This often leads to modular design where a core inference engine remains untouched, but pre-processing modules, threshold settings, and output wrappers are context specific. This allows for consistency where it matters (model logic) and flexibility where it's needed (data handling, interface logic).

Scalability also depends on feedback loops. In small deployments, developers can manually inspect outputs and tune accordingly. On a scale, that's impossible. Instead, telemetry must be built into the platform. Continuous monitoring of input distributions, output confidence, and model drift enables systems to self-asses. In mature environments, retraining can be triggered automatically when performance dips or data shifts. Feedback isn't just a nice-to-have, it's fuel for resilience.

Yet perhaps the most important and least technical requirement for scaling is clarity of purpose. Intelligent systems grow in unpredictable ways. They attract new stakeholders, gather new data, and face new scrutiny. If their original goals are not clearly defined, they risk being pulled in too many directions. Purpose anchors scale. It helps teams decide what to preserve, what to adapt, and what to say no to. Systems that try to do everything rarely do anything well.

In sum, scaling an intelligent system from prototype to platform is not a sprint, it's a reinvention. It requires a shift in priorities, architecture, governance, and mindset. It demands systems that are not just high-performing but high-integrity. It demands infrastructure that is not just efficient but ethical. And above all, it demands that we see scale not as a technical upgrade but as a deeper commitment to context, continuity, and care.

With the right foundation, a prototype can become more than a solution. It can become an ecosystem, one that grows, learns, and continues to deliver insight across the messy, beautiful, and unpredictable terrain of the real world.

Deploying an intelligent system into the wild means inviting unpredictability. Data arrives late. APIs break. User behavior shifts. And when systems fail because they inevitably will, it is not just functionality that breaks. Trust breaks. Trust is what allows users, stakeholders, and engineers to lean on a system, depend on it, and expect it to behave consistently in the face of change. It is not something that gets tacked on in the final sprint before release. It must be engineered from day one.

A truly intelligent system is not only measured by how smart its algorithms are, but by how gracefully it handles the unexpected. Trust is engineered through layers: through security, through observability, and through redundancy. Each layer acts as a reinforcement, not just for system health but for the relationship between the system and its users.

Security is the first wall. Intelligent systems often operate on sensitive data, financial records, personal health information, and behavioral signals. These datasets are not merely assets; they are liabilities if mishandled. The architecture must prioritize encryption, authentication, and access control. Every pipeline stage from ingestion, transformation, inference, storage must be secured. Secrets must be vaulted. Logs must be scrubbed. And every input must be treated as potentially malicious. Building secure-by-default systems isn't paranoid, it's prudent.

Yet technical security alone does not protect against every failure. That's where observability becomes vital. A system that cannot see itself cannot protect itself. It is not enough to know that something has gone wrong. The system must reveal what, where, and why. Metrics, logs, and traces together form the trinity of modern observability. They must be designed intentionally. Metrics track model performance, system latency, error rates, and data freshness. Logs capture the context of what the system was doing and what it saw. Traces follow requests across services, mapping journeys from frontend interaction to backend computation.

In practice, this means integrating tools like Prometheus, Grafana, Open Telemetry, and custom-built dashboards. But it also means building a culture where observability is not viewed as overhead, but as armor. Teams should be able to answer: What happened just before that spike in errors? Which feature pipeline failed? Did model predictions degrade before or after the deployment of the new version?

This continuous introspection is what separates brittle systems from resilient ones. When monitoring systems are passive, failures propagate in silence. But when monitoring systems are active when they notify, visualize, and learn they form a protective layer that detects issues before users do.

Redundancy is the final shield. It is what allows systems to degrade gracefully instead of catastrophically. Redundancy can mean horizontal scaling, where multiple model replicas share the load. It can mean fallback models, simpler algorithms that take over when complex systems go offline. It can mean caching recent predictions or precomputing responses for common inputs. The goal is not to eliminate failure, but to ensure that failure does not compromise the system's core promise to the user.

Consider an automated underwriting engine for digital loans. In normal operation, the system uses a real-time model that analyzes credit history, transaction data, and behavioral signals. But during peak traffic, inference may lag. A redundant path kicks in, rules-based heuristics that handle low-risk applications automatically while queuing complex ones for model-based review. From the user's perspective, the system remains responsive. Internally, it absorbs strain and prevents collapse.

Redundancy also applies to data ingestion. Real-time systems must be designed to handle delayed streams, missing packets, and out-of-order records. Message queues, checkpointing mechanisms, and idempotent processing logic ensure that even under stress, the system does not lose integrity.

To engineer trust is to anticipate betrayal. Every component is a candidate for failure. Every API is a handshake that might be dropped. Systems of trust are built by asking, "What happens if these breaks?" and then designing the answer into the architecture. This mindset shifts teams from reactive firefighting to proactive design.

It also influences how teams are structured. Reliable systems are not built by brilliant individuals, they are maintained by teams that share ownership, rotate responsibilities, and document tribal knowledge. Runbooks are created not for compliance, but for continuity. Chaos engineering exercises are run not for drama, but for confidence.

Ultimately, systems of trust are not just technical achievements, they are social contracts. When a user relies on a predictive system to recommend a medication, flag a financial anomaly, or guide a hiring decision, they are placing trust in more than code. They are trusting the process, the people, and the principles behind that system. To honor that trust, the system must be ready not just to succeed, but to fail with dignity.

This is what separates good systems from great ones. Not just the ability to function when conditions are perfect, but the resilience to serve when the world is messy, delayed, or broken. Security, observability, and redundancy form the foundation of this resilience. Together, they create intelligent systems that not only deliver value but deserve the trust they are given.

When an intelligent system succeeds in one environment, the natural impulse is to expand it to others. But what works in one context often fails in another not because the model is broken, but because the context is. Scaling across geographies, industries, or demographics exposes a truth often overlooked in the rush to replicate success: intelligence is not universally portable. It must be adapted.

Every data model is built with assumptions. These assumptions are shaped by culture, behavior, infrastructure, and regulation. They are often invisible until they are violated. A fraud detection algorithm trained on digital banking activity in Lagos might misclassify transactions in Kano simply because behavioral norms differ. A credit scoring model optimized for salaried workers may penalize informal traders who operate without bank accounts. These aren't edge cases, they are entire communities misrepresented by a system that was never tuned for them.

Adaptability begins with humility. Designers must ask not, "How can we scale this model?" but "What does this new context demand of us?" Local relevance is not a constraint to be managed; it is a dimension to be respected. It requires teams to go beyond the numbers and study the human environments behind them. What payment methods are most trusted? What languages dominate digital communication? How is data stored, shared, or avoided altogether?

One illustrative case comes from the deployment of an agricultural yield forecasting system. Originally piloted in South Africa, the model used satellite imagery, soil data, and weather forecasts to help farmers plan planting cycles. When the system was expanded to West Africa, performance dropped sharply. The reason? Crop types varied, local planting calendars were different, and soil characteristics weren't represented accurately in the original feature set. The model didn't fail because it was poorly built, it failed because it was misaligned. Success came only after the team incorporated local agronomic data, worked with extension officers, and rebuilt portions of the model to reflect new environmental truths.

Adaptability also demands a shift in data strategy. In emerging markets, digital data may be sparse or unstructured. Relying exclusively on web logs or financial histories creates blind spots. Teams must find alternative signals, cooperative membership, mobile airtime purchases, voice call patterns, informal surveys. These proxies, while noisy, often capture dimensions of behavior overlooked by traditional data sources. Incorporating them requires experimentation, local partnerships, and above all, trust.

Ethical adaptability matters just as much. In regions with weaker data protection laws, the temptation to scrape, mine, or infer sensitive information is higher. But deploying intelligent systems without ethical alignment can breed backlash. Communities may reject what they don't understand or what they feel misuses their data. To scale responsibly, teams must localize their ethical frameworks too. Consent, explainability, and accountability must be reinterpreted through cultural lenses. A model isn't truly global unless it respects local dignity.

Language is another fault line. Intelligent systems trained on English-language datasets often perform poorly in multilingual environments. Direct translations miss nuance. Sentiment shifts. Intent changes. A chatbot trained on Western customer service patterns may sound robotic or even disrespectful in other cultures. Adaptation here means training local corporations, collaborating with linguists, and allowing for regional slang, idioms, and tone shifts.

Regulation creates further complexity. What is allowed in one jurisdiction may be illegal in another. Data localization laws, algorithmic accountability mandates, and fairness requirements all differ. Scalable systems must be designed with modular compliance in mind. Legal, security, and operational layers must be separable and tunable. A one-size-fits-all approach will not survive scrutiny.

Yet amid all this variation, certain patterns emerge. Some system components can remain stable, core inference logic, performance monitoring, feedback mechanisms. Others must flex, feature engineering, UI/UX, language support. The art of adaptability lies in knowing which is which. In modular design, teams define what travels and what adapts. They build systems with plug-and-play components tailored to local needs.

But adaptability is not just technical. It is institutional. It means hiring local talent, building local partnerships, and giving regional teams autonomy to evolve the product. It means listening more than dictating. The most successful intelligent systems aren't those that scale *despite* difference, they are those that scale *through* it.

This is the paradox of scale: the more a system expands, the more it must specialize. Mass impact comes not from rigid replication, but from flexible reinvention. A truly intelligent system doesn't just survive new environments; it learns from them. It grows sharper, wiser, and more inclusive. That's not just scale. That's evolution.

The success of an intelligent system is never final. Even when it performs well, makes accurate predictions, and drives value for users, the world around it doesn't stand still. New behaviors emerge, regulations change, competitors adapt, and data distributions evolve in subtle but consequential ways. A model that performs beautifully today may degrade silently tomorrow. This is why, at scale, intelligent systems must be built not only to think but to learn and to learn continually, safely, and ethically.

In the early stages of development, learning is often manual. Engineers review results, observe errors, and tweak models accordingly. Feedback comes from internal tests, stakeholder reviews, and domain experts. But once a system is live, especially in environments with thousands or millions of interactions, that manual loop becomes insufficient. The system must begin to absorb feedback from the world it operates in by detecting shifts, assessing performance, and, where appropriate, adapting itself.

This is the foundation of intelligent feedback loops. At their core, they enable a system to monitor its own performance, understand the consequences of its predictions, and incorporate insights from outcomes. But at scale, feedback loops are far more complex than simple retraining mechanisms. They are the circulatory system of learning, routing insight from users, edge cases, operational environments, and failures back into the heart of the system's logic.

The challenge is not just building these loops but building them well. Poorly designed feedback loops can introduce bias, accelerate model drift, or create self-reinforcing systems that optimize for engagement over accuracy or fairness. For example, consider a content recommendation system that adapts based on user clicks. If it's not carefully regulated, it may quickly converge on sensationalist or homogenous content, amplifying polarization and reducing diversity not because the system is broken, but because it's learning from narrow signals.

To prevent such spirals, effective feedback loops must begin with clear intent. What kind of feedback matters? From whom? And how should it be interpreted? Clicks might indicate interest, or they might reflect misleading headlines. Loan approval rejections might highlight model errors, or they might signal regulatory misalignment. Feedback is not neutral. It must be filtered, contextualized, and weighed before it becomes fuel for change.

There are several types of feedback mechanisms, each with its own strengths and risks. Direct feedback includes user ratings, corrections, or flags which are explicit signals that reflect human judgment. Indirect feedback involves behavioral data: whether users abandon a page, follow a recommendation, or return to the platform. Implicit feedback requires interpretation, while explicit feedback can be sparse or biased. Intelligent systems must blend these sources carefully, calibrating their influence.

Operational feedback, meanwhile, comes from system telemetry: latency metrics, failure rates, memory usage, and throughput. These technical signals don't tell us whether a prediction is "good" in the human sense, but they reveal whether the system is healthy, scalable, and performant. A recommendation model that delivers useful results but causes memory spikes under load is a feedback issue even if the user is satisfied.

Then there's labeled feedback, the gold standard for retraining but also the hardest to obtain. In supervised learning, labeled outcomes (e.g., whether a loan was repaid or whether a medical diagnosis was correct) form the backbone of model improvement. But in the real world, these outcomes often arrive late, incompletely, or noisily. Systems must be designed to store and reconnect outcomes with original predictions, sometimes months later. This lineage, or prediction history, is vital for continuous learning.

One of the most powerful practices in large-scale learning systems is shadow deployment. Here, new models or logic are run alongside live systems, making predictions that are not shown to users but compared with actual outcomes. This allows for safe experimentation and validation without risking user trust. Feedback loops in shadow mode provide early warning signs of degradation, improvement, or bias before going live.

Another emerging practice is counterfactual feedback. Instead of only learning from what happened, systems learn from what *could have* happened. In ad delivery, for instance, a model may learn not just from served ads and clicks, but from randomly withheld alternatives. These counterfactuals help systems avoid optimizing too narrowly based on their own influence, a problem known as echo learning.

Yet, for all their promise, feedback loops can become dangerous if left ungoverned. One of the greatest risks is feedback contamination, where a system's own predictions begin to shape the data, it learns from. Consider a hiring algorithm that scores candidates. If its predictions influence who gets interviewed and hired, then the data used for future training becomes skewed. Candidates the model rejected are never interviewed so their true value remains unknown. Over time, the system may become overconfident in its biases.

This is why feedback loops must be designed not just for learning, but for controlled learning. Guardrails must be established. Performance must be monitored not only in aggregate but across subgroups. Drift must be measured not just in overall accuracy, but in distributional fairness. And human oversight must remain part of the loop not as a backup, but as a parallel intelligence.

In highly regulated industries, feedback loops must also comply with legal and ethical frameworks. For example, financial systems in many countries must not discriminate based on protected attributes like race or gender. If a model learns from biased feedback, it may unknowingly reinforce disparities. Bias audits, fairness constraints, and explainability mechanisms have become vital. They ensure that learning does not come at the cost of justice.

Governance is key here. Feedback loops at scale cannot be trusted to run on autopilot. Organizations must define who has the authority to update models, review feedback sources, and intervene in cases of harm. They must log changes, document rationale, and build internal tools for auditing decisions. This is not bureaucracy, it is maturity.

The cultural dimension is also essential. Teams must foster a learning mindset not just in the machines they build, but in themselves. Postmortems, incident reviews, and continuous evaluation processes should be part of daily operations. When a model fails, the goal is not blamed but understanding. When a signal degrades, the question is not why it broke but what it teaches.

In production environments, effective feedback loops often combine automation and human input. Automated pipelines ingest data, track performance, and trigger retraining jobs. Human reviewers validate edge cases, analyze anomalies, and adjust parameters. Together, they create a system that is both responsive and responsible.

One real-world example comes from customer service automation. A voice assistant deployed at scale to handle support calls learns continuously from interactions. It analyzes phrasing patterns, response success, call outcomes, and user sentiment. But it also allows users to opt out and leave detailed feedback. Customer service agents can annotate failed conversations. Engineers can review recordings. Feedback loops here involve a full ecosystem from users, frontline workers, data scientists, and quality analysts all contributing to a smarter, more respectful system.

But learning at scale is not just about speed or accuracy. It's about sustainability. A system that learns too quickly may be overfit with noise. One that learns too slowly may drift into irrelevance. Feedback loops must be calibrated, monitored, and tuned over time. They are not mechanical gears; they are dynamic conversations between system and world.

The most effective systems treat feedback as a dialogue. They signal uncertainty when confidence is low. They ask for clarification when inputs are ambiguous. They offer explanations that invite critique. In doing so, they don't just learn more, they teach users how to contribute meaningfully. This bi-directional trust is what separates adaptive tools from black-box automation.

As artificial intelligence becomes more embedded in everyday life, the ability to learn at scale will define which systems endure and which fade. But learning alone is not enough. Systems must be learned wisely, ethically, and transparently. They must not only respond to the world, but they must also *respect* it. Feedback is not a hack. It is not a post-launch patch or an optimization technique. It is the foundation of living systems. And when it is designed with care, governed with integrity, and executed with humility, it becomes more than a feature, it becomes a philosophy.

In this view, intelligent systems are not just machines that get better. They are systems that stay honest. Listen deeply. That change when change is needed and hold firm when it is not. Feedback, then, is not just how systems evolve, it is how they earn their place in a world that demands both intelligence and integrity.

CHAPTER 5

In the landscape of modern AI, where complex models generate decisions that affect lives, livelihoods, and entire industries, one quality stands above technical performance: interpretability. It is no longer enough for a system to be accurate; it must be intelligible. Users, regulators, stakeholders, and the general public all need to understand not only what a system predicts but why it does so. Without this clarity, trust crumbles, adoption stalls, and intelligent systems become fragile tools wielded with uncertainty.

Interpretability, at its core, is about bridging the cognitive gap between algorithmic complexity and human comprehension. It involves designing models, tools, and interfaces that allow people to grasp how inputs relate to outputs. It is not about dumbing things down. It is about lifting others up, giving them the conceptual handles needed to interact meaningfully with intelligence that might otherwise feel opaque.

In early machine learning systems, interpretability was a byproduct. Simpler models like decision trees, logistic regression, or rule-based classifiers were inherently interpretable. You could inspect weights, trace rules, and explain outcomes in natural language. But as the field advanced, the hunger for performance drove systems into higher dimensions. Deep neural networks, ensemble methods, and transformer-based architectures began outperforming their simpler counterparts but at a cost. Their internal workings became too complex to explain directly, giving rise to the era of the black box.

Black-box models pose a serious challenge in domains where accountability is non-negotiable. In healthcare, where an AI diagnosis might inform treatment, a doctor needs to understand the rationale. In finance, where a model declines a loan application, applicants and regulators alike demand justification. In criminal justice, where risk assessments influence sentencing or bail, opaque predictions are not just unethical, they can be unconstitutional.

The question then becomes: how can we maintain performance while recovering interpretability? This tension has birthed a growing field of research and practice focused on explainable AI (XAI). But within this field, two distinct approaches emerge. The first is to build inherently interpretable models, simpler, structured systems that offer transparency by design. The second is to apply interpretability techniques to complex models after they are trained.

Inherently interpretable models are preferred in high-stakes environments with well-understood variables. These include linear models, decision lists, and generalized additive models. Their strength lies in their alignment with human reasoning. You can trace a prediction, examine individual features, and reproduce behavior. But these models often lack the expressive power needed for noisy or high-dimensional data.

For more complex systems, post hoc explanations are used. Techniques like LIME (Local Interpretable Model-agnostic Explanations) and SHAP (SHapley Additive exPlanations) aim to interpret model outputs by approximating local behavior. LIME creates a simple model that mimics the complex model's predictions around a specific input. SHAP values, inspired by game theory, assign important scores to features by measuring how much each one contributes to the final prediction.

These tools are powerful, but they are not without limitations. Their explanations are approximations, not ground truths. They help us interpret, but they do not fully reveal the model's logic. Moreover, they can be gamed or misunderstood if not used carefully. This is why interpretability is not merely a technical problem; it is a communication challenge. It demands clarity, nuance, and empathy.

Communication design plays a vital role here. Dashboards, visualizations, and report generators must present explanations in ways that are digestible, accurate, and actionable. For business analysts, a breakdown of feature weights might suffice. For consumers, natural language narratives may be better. For regulators, audit logs and decision trees could be essential. The same explanation cannot serve all audiences.

My career reflects a deep understanding of this challenge. In his work deploying AI-driven infrastructure across sectors, he consistently emphasizes not just the accuracy of the models, but their communicability. In one project, designed to streamline digital credit assessment, the model was built with SHAP-based explanation layers that translated prediction results into reason codes. Borrowers didn't just see a decision, they saw why it was made: "low transaction consistency," "recent overdraft activity," or "incomplete KYC documentation."

This layer of transparency had a profound effect. Approval rates became easier to contest or justify. Customer service agents could interpret decisions without needing to consult engineers. More importantly, users felt respected. When systems explain themselves, they become partners, not judges.

But interpretability extends beyond one-off explanations. In dynamic systems like recommendation engines or fraud detection pipelines models evolve continuously. Interpretability must evolve with them. This means versioning explanations alongside models, tracking changes in feature importance, and embedding interpretability into the development lifecycle.

There's also a growing movement toward counterfactual explanation. Instead of simply stating why a prediction was made, these systems answer the question, "What would need to change for a different outcome?" For example, "Your loan application was declined. If your monthly income were NGN 30,000 higher, it would have been approved." Counterfactuals empower users by giving them an agency, they move the conversation from justification to action.

Still, caution is required. Explanations can create a false sense of understanding. They can be too simplistic, too technical, or misleadingly confident. A model that says "You were declined because of your location" may be correct but that information, if misused, could violate laws or ethical norms. This is why organizations must not only build interpretable systems but govern them. Ethics committees, bias audits, and human-in-the-loop review processes are essential checks.

Interpretability also plays a role in team dynamics. Data scientists, engineers, and business stakeholders often speak different languages. Explanatory tools become bridges across disciplines. They help translate model logic into business KPIs. They inform UI/UX decisions. They reveal gaps in data collection. In short, they turn machine learning from a technical artifact into a shared conversation.

In education, interpretability fosters learning. Junior data scientists gain intuition by inspecting feature attributions. Non-technical teams become empowered to question assumptions. As models become more democratized via AutoML tools or no-code platforms, interpretability ensures that power does not outpaced responsibility.

The future of intelligent systems depends on interpretability not as a feature, but as a foundation. Systems that cannot be understood cannot be trusted. Systems that cannot be challenged cannot be improved. And systems that hide their reasoning risk not just technical failure, but societal harm.

To design for understanding is to honor the human in the loop. It is to recognize that intelligence must be legible, that decisions must be explainable, and that clarity is as important as correctness. In doing so, we don't just build better systems, we build better relationships between people and machines.

And in an age where intelligence shapes everything from loans to life, those relationships matter more than ever.

When an intelligent system succeeds in one environment, the natural impulse is to expand it to others. But what works in one context often fails in another not because the model is broken, but because the context is. Scaling across geographies, industries, or demographics exposes a truth often overlooked in the rush to replicate success: intelligence is not universally portable. It must be adapted.

Every data model is built with assumptions. These assumptions are shaped by culture, behavior, infrastructure, and regulation. They are often invisible until they are violated. A fraud detection algorithm trained on digital banking activity in Lagos might misclassify transactions in Kano simply because behavioral norms differ. A credit scoring model optimized for salaried workers may penalize informal traders who operate without bank accounts. These aren't edge cases, they are entire communities misrepresented by a system that was never tuned for them.

Adaptability begins with humility. Designers must ask not, "How can we scale this model?" but "What does this new context demand of us?" Local relevance is not a constraint to be managed; it is a dimension to be respected. It requires teams to go beyond the numbers and study the human environments behind them. What payment methods are most trusted? What languages dominate digital communication? How is data stored, shared, or avoided altogether?

One illustrative case comes from the deployment of an agricultural yield forecasting system. Originally piloted in South Africa, the model used satellite imagery, soil data, and weather forecasts to help farmers plan planting cycles. When the system was expanded to West Africa, performance dropped sharply. The reason? Crop types varied, local planting calendars were different, and soil characteristics weren't represented accurately in the original feature set. The model didn't fail because it was poorly built, it failed because it was misaligned. Success came only after the team incorporated local agronomic data, worked with extension officers, and rebuilt portions of the model to reflect new environmental truths.

Adaptability also demands a shift in data strategy. In emerging markets, digital data may be sparse or unstructured. Relying exclusively on web logs or financial histories creates blind spots. Teams must find alternative signals from cooperative membership, mobile airtime purchases, voice call patterns, informal surveys. These proxies, while noisy, often capture dimensions of behavior overlooked by traditional data sources. Incorporating them requires experimentation, local partnerships, and above all, trust.

Ethical adaptability matters just as much. In regions with weaker data protection laws, the temptation to scrape, mine, or infer sensitive information is higher. But deploying intelligent systems without ethical alignment can breed backlash. Communities may reject what they don't understand or what they feel misuses their data. To scale responsibly, teams must localize their ethical frameworks too. Consent, explainability, and accountability must be reinterpreted through cultural lenses. A model isn't truly global unless it respects local dignity.

Language is another fault line. Intelligent systems trained on English-language datasets often perform poorly in multilingual environments. Direct translations miss nuance. Sentiment shifts. Intent changes. A chatbot trained on Western customer service patterns may sound robotic or even disrespectful in other cultures. Adaptation here means training local corporations, collaborating with linguists, and allowing for regional slang, idioms, and tone shifts.

Regulation creates further complexity. What is allowed in one jurisdiction may be illegal in another. Data localization laws, algorithmic accountability mandates, and fairness requirements all differ. Scalable systems must be designed with modular compliance in mind. Legal, security, and operational layers must be separable and tunable. A one-size-fits-all approach will not survive scrutiny.

The power of artificial intelligence is not solely in its predictive strength or computational sophistication. Its real power lies in its capacity to empower people, those who rely on it, interact with it, and build upon it. For AI to be impactful, it must be intelligible, but beyond that, it must be usable. The path from insight to action is bridged by one essential design challenge: the interface.

In traditional software design, interfaces are often thought of as screens, dashboards, and forms. In the context of AI, however, an interface is more than a medium, it is a relationship. It is how intelligence speaks to people, and how people, in turn, query, challenge, and rely on that intelligence. A well-designed interface transforms abstract intelligence into usable, tangible insight. A poor interface, on the other hand, can render even the most advanced system irrelevant.

If interfaces obscure this uncertainty, users may either over-trust or under-trust the system. Both are dangerous. By clearly communicating confidence levels, ranges, or alternative options, interfaces help users calibrate their trust appropriately. In doing so, they foster not only usage but responsibility.

In the landscape of modern AI, where complex models generate decisions that affect lives, livelihoods, and entire industries, one quality stands above technical performance: interpretability. It is no longer enough for a system to be accurate; it must be intelligible. Users, regulators, stakeholders, and the general public all need to understand not only what a system predicts but why it does so. Without this clarity, trust crumbles, adoption stalls, and intelligent systems become fragile tools wielded with uncertainty.

Interpretability, at its core, is about bridging the cognitive gap between algorithmic complexity and human comprehension. It involves designing models, tools, and interfaces that allow people to grasp how inputs relate to outputs. It is not about dumbing things down. It is about lifting others up, giving them the conceptual handles needed to interact meaningfully with intelligence that might otherwise feel opaque.

In early machine learning systems, interpretability was a byproduct. Simpler models like decision trees, logistic regression, or rule-based classifiers were inherently interpretable. You could inspect weights, trace rules, and explain outcomes in natural language. But as the field advanced, the hunger for performance drove systems into higher dimensions. Deep neural networks, ensemble methods, and transformer-based architectures began outperforming their simpler counterparts but at a cost. Their internal workings became too complex to explain directly, giving rise to the era of the black box.

Black-box models pose a serious challenge in domains where accountability is non-negotiable. In healthcare, where an AI diagnosis might inform treatment, a doctor needs to understand the rationale. In finance, where a model declines a loan application, applicants and regulators alike demand justification. In criminal justice, where risk assessments influence sentencing or bail, opaque predictions are not just unethical, they can be unconstitutional.

The question then becomes: how can we maintain performance while recovering interpretability? This tension has birthed a growing field of research and practice focused on explainable AI (XAI). But within this field, two distinct approaches emerge. The first is to build inherently interpretable models to be simpler, structured systems that offer transparency by design. The second is to apply interpretability techniques to complex models after they are trained.

Inherently interpretable models are preferred in high-stakes environments with well-understood variables. These include linear models, decision lists, and generalized additive models. Their strength lies in their alignment with human reasoning. You can trace a prediction, examine individual features, and reproduce behavior. But these models often lack the expressive power needed for noisy or high-dimensional data.

This layer of transparency had a profound effect. Approval rates became easier to contest or justify. Customer service agents could interpret decisions without needing to consult engineers. More importantly, users felt respected. When systems explain themselves, they become partners, not judges.

But interpretability extends beyond one-off explanations. In dynamic systems like recommendation engines or fraud detection pipelines models evolve continuously. Interpretability must evolve with them. This means versioning explanations alongside models, tracking changes in feature importance, and embedding interpretability into the development lifecycle.

There's also a growing movement toward counterfactual explanation. Instead of simply stating why a prediction was made, these systems answer the question, "What would need to change for a different outcome?" For example, "Your loan application was declined. If your monthly income were NGN 30,000 higher, it would have been approved." Counterfactuals empower users by giving them an agency, they move the conversation from justification to action.

Still, caution is required. Explanations can create a false sense of understanding. They can be too simplistic, too technical, or misleadingly confident. A model that says "You were declined because of your location" may be correct but that information, if misused, could violate laws or ethical norms. This is why organizations must not only build interpretable systems but govern them. Ethics committees, bias audits, and human-in-the-loop review processes are essential checks.

Interpretability also plays a role in team dynamics. Data scientists, engineers, and business stakeholders often speak different languages. Explanatory tools become bridges across disciplines. They help translate model logic into business KPIs. They inform UI/UX decisions. They reveal gaps in data collection. In short, they turn machine learning from a technical artifact into a shared conversation.

In education, interpretability fosters learning. Junior data scientists gain intuition by inspecting feature attributions. Non-technical teams become empowered to question assumptions. As models become more democratized via AutoML tools or no-code platforms, interpretability ensures that power does not outpaced responsibility.

The future of intelligent systems depends on interpretability not as a feature, but as a foundation. Systems that cannot be understood cannot be trusted. Systems that cannot be challenged cannot be improved. And systems that hide their reasoning risk not just technical failure, but societal harm.

To design for understanding is to honor the human in the loop. It is to recognize that intelligence must be legible, that decisions must be explainable, and that clarity is as important as correctness. In doing so, we don't just build better systems, we build better relationships between people and machines. And in an age where intelligence shapes everything from loans to life, those relationships matter more than ever.

The success of an intelligent system is never final. Even when it performs well, makes accurate predictions, and drives value for users, the world around it doesn't stand still. New behaviors emerge, regulations change, competitors adapt, and data distributions evolve in subtle but consequential ways. A model that performs beautifully today may degrade silently tomorrow. This is why, on a scale, intelligent systems must be built not only to think but to learn and to learn continually, safely, and ethically.

In the early stages of development, learning is often manual. Engineers review results, observe errors, and tweak models accordingly. Feedback comes from internal tests, stakeholder reviews, and domain experts. But once a system is live, especially in environments with thousands or millions of interactions, that manual loop becomes insufficient. The system must begin to absorb feedback from the world it operates in by detecting shifts, assessing performance, and, where appropriate, adapting itself.

This is the foundation of intelligent feedback loops. At their core, they enable a system to monitor its own performance, understand the consequences of its predictions, and incorporate insights from outcomes. But at scale, feedback loops are far more complex than simple retraining mechanisms. They are the circulatory system of learning, routing insight from users, edge cases, operational environments, and failures back into the heart of the system's logic.

The challenge is not just building these loops but building them well. Poorly designed feedback loops can introduce bias, accelerate model drift, or create self-reinforcing systems that optimize for engagement over accuracy or fairness. For example, consider a content recommendation system that adapts based on user clicks. If it's not carefully regulated, it may quickly converge on sensationalist or homogenous content, amplifying polarization and reducing diversity not because the system is broken, but because it's learning from narrow signals.

To prevent such spirals, effective feedback loops must begin with clear intent. What kind of feedback matters? From whom? And how should it be interpreted? Clicks might indicate interest, or they might reflect misleading headlines. Loan approval rejections might highlight model errors, or they might signal regulatory misalignment. Feedback is not neutral. It must be filtered, contextualized, and weighed before it becomes fuel for change.

There are several types of feedback mechanisms, each with its own strengths and risks. Direct feedback includes user ratings, corrections, or flags explicit signals that reflect human judgment. Indirect feedback involves behavioral data: whether users abandon a page, follow a recommendation, or return to the platform. Implicit feedback requires interpretation, while explicit feedback can be sparse or biased. Intelligent systems must blend these sources carefully, calibrating their influence.

Operational feedback, meanwhile, comes from system telemetry: latency metrics, failure rates, memory usage, and throughput. These technical signals don't tell us whether a prediction is "good" in the human sense, but they reveal whether the system is healthy, scalable, and performant. A recommendation model that delivers useful results but causes memory spikes under load is a feedback issue even if the user is satisfied.

Then there's labeled feedback, the gold standard for retraining but also the hardest to obtain. In supervised learning, labeled outcomes (e.g., whether a loan was repaid or whether a medical diagnosis was correct) form the backbone of model improvement. But in the real world, these outcomes often arrive late, incompletely, or noisily. Systems must be designed to store and reconnect outcomes with original predictions, sometimes months later. This lineage, or prediction history, is vital for continuous learning.

One of the most powerful practices in large-scale learning systems is shadow deployment. Here, new models or logic are run alongside live systems, making predictions that are not shown to users but compared with actual outcomes. This allows for safe experimentation and validation without risking user trust. Feedback loops in shadow mode provide early warning signs of degradation, improvement, or bias before going live.

Another emerging practice is counterfactual feedback. Instead of only learning from what happened, systems learn from what *could have* happened. In ad delivery, for instance, a model may learn not just from served ads and clicks, but from randomly withheld alternatives. These counterfactuals help systems avoid optimizing too narrowly based on their own influence, a problem known as echo learning.

Yet, for all their promise, feedback loops can become dangerous if left ungoverned. One of the greatest risks is feedback contamination, where a system's own predictions begin to shape the data it learns from. Consider a hiring algorithm that scores candidates. If its predictions influence who gets interviewed and hired, then the data used for future training becomes skewed. Candidates the model rejected are never interviewed so their true value remains unknown. Over time, the system may become overconfident in its biases.

This is why feedback loops must be designed not just for learning, but for controlled learning. Guardrails must be established. Performance must be monitored not only in aggregate but across subgroups. Drift must be measured not just in overall accuracy, but in distributional fairness. And human oversight must remain part of the loop not as a backup, but as a parallel intelligence.

In highly regulated industries, feedback loops must also comply with legal and ethical frameworks. For example, financial systems in many countries must not discriminate based on protected attributes like race or gender. If a model learns from biased feedback, it may unknowingly reinforce disparities. Bias audits, fairness constraints, and explainability mechanisms have become vital. They ensure that learning does not come at the cost of justice.

A fraud detection algorithm trained on digital banking activity in Lagos might misclassify transactions in Kano simply because behavioral norms differ. A credit scoring model optimized for salaried workers may penalize informal traders who operate without bank accounts. These aren't edge cases, they are entire communities misrepresented by a system that was never tuned for them. Language is another fault line. Intelligent systems trained on English-language datasets often perform poorly in multilingual environments. Direct translations miss nuance. Sentiment shifts. Intent changes. A chatbot trained on Western customer service patterns may sound robotic or even disrespectful in other cultures. Adaptation here means training local corporations, collaborating with linguists, and allowing for regional slang, idioms, and tone shifts.

Trust is the foundation of every meaningful interaction between humans and machines. In the context of artificial intelligence and data-driven decision-making, trust is not merely a soft sentiment, it is a critical determinant of adoption, effectiveness, and sustainability. If users do not trust the systems they are expected to rely on, those systems will either be ignored or resisted. But trust in AI is fragile, particularly when predictions come wrapped in layers of abstraction and statistical ambiguity. And nothing threatens that trust more than perceived bias or false certainty.

Artificial intelligence, by design, is probabilistic. Models do not deliver facts; they deliver predictions with degrees of confidence. Yet too often, these predictions are presented with the weight of finality. A model might estimate a 93% likelihood that a customer will churn or a 70% probability of loan default, but to the end-user, this often reads as a binary conclusion. This miscommunication between probability and certainty is where trust can erode.

Bias, however, remains a more insidious threat to trust. AI models trained on historical data can easily learn the biases embedded in that data whether those biases stem from social inequality, reporting errors, or systemic discrimination. A hiring model trained on resumes from past hires may learn to favor men over women. A predictive policing tool trained on arrest data may reinforce racial profiling. And a loan approval model that draws from financial histories may exclude those who've never had access to formal banking.

Users intuitively recognize when systems feel unfair, even if they cannot articulate the technical flaws. And when they sense bias, especially when that bias affects high-stakes outcomes like employment, healthcare, or legal judgment, trust vanishes. It's not enough for models to be accurate; they must be fair. And fairness is not a technical metric alone; it is a lived experience.

This is why designing for trust requires a multi-dimensional approach. It begins with rigorous audits of model inputs and outputs. Are certain groups consistently disadvantaged? Do small changes in sensitive variables like race, gender, or age result in large shifts in predictions? Tools like fairness indicators, disparate impact analysis, and counterfactual fairness models can help expose these dynamics. But numbers alone don't repair trust.

Trust is also rebuilt through inclusion. Diverse teams are less likely to build systems that blindly replicate their own biases. Including domain experts, ethicists, and community representatives in the development process helps surface blind spots early. Engaging users in co-design ensures that systems are not just technically sound but culturally competent.

Equally important is how systems handle ambiguity. Not every input yields a confident prediction. Not every question has a clear answer. In such cases, AI systems should signal their uncertainty, defer to human judgment, or seek additional input. Overconfidence whether in tone or behavior is one of the quickest ways to break trust. Users can handle ambiguity. What they resent is being misled.

This principle is especially critical in public sector applications. When a government uses AI to distribute benefits, flag tax anomalies, or allocate police resources, it must be clear about the role AI plays. Is the system advisory or determinative? Can users appeal? Are decisions auditable? Transparency here is not optional, it is a democratic necessity. My work in designing explainable models consistently prioritizes this kind of trust architecture. He has advocated layered explainability where basic users see intuitive summaries, while technical users can drill down into the statistical logic. He has also pushed for dynamic explanation interfaces that adapt to user expertise and context.

But even the most carefully designed interfaces cannot overcome a core issue: users do not trust what they do not feel in control of. That's why trust also depends on agency. Can users challenge the system? Can they provide additional data? Can they opt out? Systems that invite user feedback, correction, or override build a sense of shared control. Those that do not risk being perceived as authoritarian, even if well-intentioned.

Language remains central throughout. Whether in pop-ups, dashboards, voice assistants, or legal disclaimers, every word carries weight. "You were denied" feels very different from "Based on current information, we could not approve your request." The former is final; the latter is conditional and that difference can mean everything.

In designing trustworthy systems, teams must engage in what some call "linguistic ethics." This means choosing not only what to say but how to say it. It means avoiding euphemisms that obscure risk. It means resisting the urge to overpromise. It means designing interfaces that reflect not just the state of the model, but the dignity of the user. Ultimately, trust in AI is not built by being flawless. It is built by being clear, fair, and responsive. It is built by systems that acknowledge their limits, that learn from feedback, and that treat people as partners, not endpoints. Bias and overconfidence are not inevitable but preventing them requires intention, vigilance, and humility.

As the presence of intelligent systems grows in daily life, the language we use to explain them becomes as important as the logic that powers them. Trust is not a byproduct of good engineering; it is a design goal. And like all design goals, it must be pursued deliberately. To earn trust is to speak carefully, act transparently, and build with integrity. That is how intelligent systems become not just tools of prediction but instruments of progress.

The power of artificial intelligence is not solely in its predictive strength or computational sophistication. Its real power lies in its capacity to empower people, those who rely on it, interact with it, and build upon it. For AI to be impactful, it must be intelligible, but beyond that, it must be usable. The path from insight to action is bridged by one essential design challenge: the interface.

In traditional software design, interfaces are often thought of as screens, dashboards, and forms. In the context of AI, however, an interface is more than a medium, it is a relationship. It is how intelligence speaks to people, and how people, in turn, query, challenge, and rely on that intelligence. A well-designed interface transforms abstract intelligence into usable, tangible insight. A poor interface, on the other hand, can render even the most advanced system irrelevant. At the heart of human-centered intelligence is the principle of accessibility. This doesn't just mean visual clarity or compliance with screen readers. It means that insights are presented in ways that match the mental models, priorities, and workflows of the humans they are meant to serve. A model's output must be translated into narratives, visualizations, or alerts that make sense to real people in real roles.

This approach to designing intelligent systems consistently centers on this principle. In projects spanning financial services, healthcare, and logistics, his teams have invested in building interfaces that respect the user's context. In one deployment, a risk-scoring algorithm for microloans was embedded within a tool used by field agents. Rather than presenting a numeric score alone, the interface included short narratives, confidence bands, and color-coded indicators that helped agents understand, trust, and explain the score to clients in informal markets.

To prevent such spirals, effective feedback loops must begin with clear intent. What kind of feedback matters? From whom? And how should it be interpreted? Clicks might indicate interest or they might reflect misleading headlines. Loan approval rejections might highlight model errors or they might signal regulatory misalignment. Feedback is not neutral. It must be filtered, contextualized, and weighed before it becomes fuel for change.

There are several types of feedback mechanisms, each with its own strengths and risks. Direct feedback includes user ratings, corrections, or flags, explicit signals that reflect human judgment. Indirect feedback involves behavioral data: whether users abandon a page, follow a recommendation, or return to the platform. Implicit feedback requires interpretation, while explicit feedback can be sparse or biased. Intelligent systems must blend these sources carefully, calibrating their influence.

Operational feedback, meanwhile, comes from system telemetry: latency metrics, failure rates, memory usage, and throughput. These technical signals don't tell us whether a prediction is "good" in the human sense, but they reveal whether the system is healthy, scalable, and performant. A recommendation model that delivers useful results but causes memory spikes under load is a feedback issue even if the user is satisfied.

Then there's labeled feedback, the gold standard for retraining but also the hardest to obtain. In supervised learning, labeled outcomes (e.g., whether a loan was repaid or whether a medical diagnosis was correct) form the backbone of model improvement. But in the real world, these outcomes often arrive late, incompletely, or noisily. Systems must be designed to store and reconnect outcomes with original predictions, sometimes months later. This lineage, or prediction history, is vital for continuous learning.

One of the most powerful practices in large-scale learning systems is shadow deployment. Here, new models or logic are run alongside live systems, making predictions that are not shown to users but compared with actual outcomes. This allows for safe experimentation and validation without risking user trust. Feedback loops in shadow mode provide early warning signs of degradation, improvement, or bias before going live.

Another emerging practice is counterfactual feedback. Instead of only learning from what happened, systems learn from what *could have* happened. In ad delivery, for instance, a model may learn not just from served ads and clicks, but from randomly withheld alternatives. These counterfactuals help systems avoid optimizing too narrowly based on their own influence, a problem known as echo learning.

Yet, for all their promise, feedback loops can become dangerous if left ungoverned. One of the greatest risks is feedback contamination, where a system's own predictions begin to shape the data, it learns from. Consider a hiring algorithm that scores candidates. If its predictions influence who gets interviewed and hired, then the data used for future training becomes skewed. Candidates the model rejected are never interviewed so their true value remains unknown. Over time, the system may become overconfident in its biases.

This is why feedback loops must be designed not just for learning, but for controlled learning. Guardrails must be established. Performance must be monitored not only in aggregate but across subgroups. Drift must be measured not just in overall accuracy, but in distributional fairness. And human oversight must remain part of the loop not as a backup, but as a parallel intelligence.

In highly regulated industries, feedback loops must also comply with legal and ethical frameworks. For example, financial systems in many countries must not discriminate based on protected attributes like race or gender. If a model learns from biased feedback, it may unknowingly reinforce disparities. Bias audits, fairness constraints, and explainability mechanisms have become vital. They ensure that learning does not come at the cost of justice.

Governance is key here. Feedback loops at scale cannot be trusted to run on autopilot. Organizations must define who has the authority to update models, review feedback sources, and intervene in cases of harm. They must log changes, document rationale, and build internal tools for auditing decisions. This is not bureaucracy, it is maturity. The cultural dimension is also essential. Teams must foster a learning mindset not just in the machines they build, but in themselves. Postmortems, incident reviews, and continuous evaluation processes should be part of daily operations.

When a model fails, the goal is not blamed but understanding. When a signal degrades, the question is not why it broke but what it teaches.

In production environments, effective feedback loops often combine automation and human input. Automated pipelines ingest data, track performance, and trigger retraining jobs. Human reviewers validate edge cases, analyze anomalies, and adjust parameters. Together, they create a system that is both responsive and responsible.

One real-world example comes from customer service automation. A voice assistant deployed at scale to handle support calls learns continuously from interactions. It analyzes phrasing patterns, response success, call outcomes, and user sentiment. But it also allows users to opt out and leave detailed feedback. Customer service agents can annotate failed conversations. Engineers can review recordings. Feedback loops here involve a full ecosystem, users, frontline workers, data scientists, and quality analysts all contributing to a smarter, more respectful system.

But learning at scale is not just about speed or accuracy. It's about sustainability. A system that learns too quickly may be overfit to noise. One that learns too slowly may drift into irrelevance. Feedback loops must be calibrated, monitored, and tuned over time. They are not mechanical gears; they are dynamic conversations between system and world.

The most effective systems treat feedback as a dialogue. They signal uncertainty when confidence is low. They ask for clarification when inputs are ambiguous. They offer explanations that invite critique. In doing so, they don't just learn more, they teach users how to contribute meaningfully. This bi-directional trust is what separates adaptive tools from black-box automation. As artificial intelligence becomes more embedded in everyday life, the ability to learn at scale will define which systems endure and which fade. But learning alone is not enough. Systems must be learned wisely, ethically, and transparently. They must not only respond to the world, but they must also *respect* it.

Feedback is not a hack. It is not a post-launch patch or an optimization technique. It is the foundation of living systems. And when it is designed with care, governed with integrity, and executed with humility, it becomes more than a feature, it becomes a philosophy.

requirements all differ. Scalable systems must be designed with modular compliance in mind. Legal, security, and operational layers must be separable and tunable. A one-size-fits-all approach will not survive scrutiny.

In today's era of data-driven innovation, the emergence of intelligent infrastructure has significantly transformed the way humans interact with the physical and digital world. The development of smart systems ranging from automated energy grids and transportation networks to digital health platforms and industrial Internet of Things (IoT) applications has brought about an unprecedented level of autonomy, efficiency, and connectivity. However, the rise of such intelligent systems also introduces new levels of complexity and vulnerability. As these systems generate and rely on vast volumes of real-time data to function effectively, they become increasingly susceptible to disruption, manipulation, and failure. At the core of protecting and sustaining these infrastructures lies the critical discipline of anomaly detection.

Anomaly detection refers to the identification of patterns, observations, or behaviors within a data stream that do not conform to expected norms. These deviations, often called outliers or irregularities, can be benign or indicative of more serious underlying issues such as hardware malfunction, data corruption, fraudulent activity, or cyber-intrusion. The ability to detect such anomalies in a timely and accurate manner is central to maintaining the trustworthiness and security of intelligent systems. Unlike traditional systems that operate within predictable constraints, smart systems are dynamic, decentralized, and highly adaptive. This makes static, rule-based monitoring approaches inadequate. As a result, anomaly detection in intelligent infrastructure must be equally dynamic, scalable, and context sensitive.

The importance of anomaly detection becomes particularly evident when examining specific sectors that rely on intelligent infrastructure. In smart energy grids, for instance, a consistent flow of real-time data is used to monitor electricity consumption, generation, and distribution. A sudden voltage fluctuation or unexpected load imbalance might signal a hardware fault or, worse, a deliberate attack on the grid's control system. By detecting such abnormalities early, grid operators can prevent cascading failures that might lead to blackouts or safety hazards. Similarly, in smart transportation networks where autonomous vehicles and traffic management systems interact in real-time, anomaly detection is crucial to identifying erratic vehicle behavior, potential routing conflicts, or even malicious interference with GPS signals. Such incidents, if undetected, could jeopardize public safety on a massive scale.

In digital healthcare, wearable medical devices and remote monitoring systems collect sensitive physiological data around the clock. An unexpected spike in heart rate, blood pressure, or glucose levels if left unnoticed can result in delayed medical response and serious health outcomes. Anomaly detection systems can provide early warnings to patients and healthcare providers, prompting swift intervention. In the domain of smart manufacturing, where production lines and machines are integrated via IoT sensors, irregularities in vibration, temperature, or torque readings might indicate mechanical degradation or misalignment. Predictive maintenance algorithms fueled by anomaly detection models can reduce equipment downtime, extend asset life, and lower operational costs.

Beneath these practical applications lies a foundation of data science techniques that enable machines to distinguish between normal and abnormal behavior. In traditional contexts, anomaly detection relied heavily on statistical approaches such as z-scores, probability distributions, and control charts. These methods function by assuming a known distribution of data and flagging instances that deviate beyond acceptable thresholds. While useful in well-defined environments, these techniques often fall short in high-dimensional and non-linear data scenarios commonly encountered in smart systems.

To address this limitation, machine learning approaches have emerged as more effective alternatives. Supervised, semi-supervised, and unsupervised learning models can learn patterns from historical data, adapt to new conditions, and generalize well across multiple contexts. Algorithms such as isolation forests, one-class support vector machines, and k-near neighbors can model the complex behavior of intelligent systems with greater flexibility. However, even these models face limitations when dealing with unstructured data, large-scale streaming information, and temporal dependencies.

The evolution of anomaly detection has thus moved into the realm of deep learning, particularly for systems requiring the analysis of time-series data or multi-dimensional inputs. Neural network architectures such as autoencoders are trained to compress and reconstruct data inputs. When a system fails to reconstruct a data point accurately, it suggests the point is anomalous. Similarly, recurrent neural networks, particularly Long Short-Term Memory (LSTM) networks, are proficient in learning temporal patterns and detecting sequential anomalies, making them ideal for real-time system monitoring. Convolutional neural networks, while traditionally used in image recognition, have also found relevance in anomaly detection tasks involving visual inspection or video surveillance in smart environments.

Despite the progress made, implementing anomaly detection in intelligent infrastructure is not without its challenges. One major obstacle is the quality and labeling of data. Real-world data is often noisy, incomplete, or imbalanced, with far fewer examples of anomalies compared to normal cases. This scarcity of labeled anomalous data complicates the training process, especially in supervised learning contexts. Many smart systems also experience dynamic behavior, meaning that what is considered normal today may become obsolete tomorrow. This problem, known as concept drift, requires models that are capable of continuous learning and adaptation.

Another issue is the difficulty in defining "normal" behavior within complex systems. Baselines can change based on time of day, environmental conditions, or user preferences. Rigid threshold-based systems are likely to produce high false positives or miss genuine threats. Adaptive models that consider contextual and environmental factors are necessary to address these dynamic baselines. Moreover, as models grow in complexity, particularly deep learning-based ones, their interpretability becomes a serious concern. Stakeholders, especially in sensitive industries such as healthcare or finance, must be able to understand and trust the decisions made by these systems. Explainability tools such as SHAP and LIME have been developed to address this, but the challenge remains unresolved on a scale.

Another pressing concern is the need for real-time performance and scalability. Intelligent systems operate at high velocity and generate data at an immense scale. Anomaly detection models must, therefore, be computationally efficient and capable of processing data with minimal latency. This has led to a rise in edge computing solutions, where data processing is conducted close to the source of generation, reducing transmission time and enabling faster response.

Drawing from my personal experience developing and deploying anomaly detection systems across sectors, I have observed several trends and insights that point toward the future of intelligent system security. First, the most effective detection systems often integrate multiple layers of analysis combining statistical preprocessing, machine learning inference, and deep learning refinement. This hybrid approach enables a more robust detection pipeline capable of handling both simple and complex anomalies.

Second, while automation is indispensable for scale, the importance of maintaining human oversight cannot be overstated. Human-in-the-loop systems where analysts are involved in validating or correcting model outputs enhance the system's learning and help mitigate the risks of false positives. Visual dashboards, annotation tools, and interactive interfaces empower experts to feed domain knowledge back into the system, thereby improving model accuracy and trustworthiness over time.

Third, the context in which anomaly detection is applied greatly influences the design of the system. A one-size-fits-all approach is unlikely to yield effective results. For example, the characteristics of an anomaly in a smart energy system may differ significantly from those in a digital banking application. Customization based on domain-specific knowledge, environmental parameters, and stakeholder needs is essential for meaningful anomaly detection.

Lastly, the ethical implications of deploying such systems must be considered from the outset. Many intelligent infrastructures operate in environments where decisions have direct consequences on human lives and rights. Surveillance systems powered by anomaly detection must strike a balance between security and privacy. Medical monitoring platforms must ensure data confidentiality while maintaining high sensitivity. Bias in training data can also lead to discriminatory outcomes, particularly when applied to systems that affect vulnerable populations. As such, ethical frameworks and regulatory compliance must be embedded in every stage of the model lifecycle from data collection and model training to deployment and monitoring.

In conclusion, anomaly detection represents one of the most powerful tools for securing intelligent infrastructure in the face of growing complexity and uncertainty. It transforms data into insight, insight into foresight, and foresight into action. By continuously monitoring the pulse of smart systems, anomaly detection enables early intervention, reduces risk, and enhances operational resilience. The journey toward fully autonomous and secure intelligent infrastructure is ongoing, but with data science, ethical oversight, and cross-disciplinary collaboration, the vision of proactive and self-defending systems is within reach.

CHAPTER 6

In the digital age, where vast amounts of personal and financial data are exchanged across interconnected platforms, fraud has emerged as a persistent and evolving threat. As economies shift increasingly toward cashless transactions and digitized services, fraudsters too have become more sophisticated, leveraging technology to exploit vulnerabilities in systems that were once considered secure. The rise of intelligent infrastructure, while offering unprecedented efficiency and access, has expanded the surface area for cybercriminals to exploit. Consequently, there is an urgent and ever-growing need to adopt predictive models capable of identifying and preventing fraud before it occurs. Predictive fraud detection rooted in data science and machine learning represents a shift from reactive incident response to proactive risk mitigation.

Fraud detection, in its simplest form, is the process of identifying illegitimate or unauthorized transactions, access, or behaviors within a system. Traditionally, this has involved static rule-based systems where predefined conditions would trigger alerts. For instance, a credit card transaction over a certain threshold in a foreign country might be flagged. However, while these systems are quick to implement and transparent in logic, they are notoriously brittle. Fraud tactics evolve, and fixed rules cannot adapt fast enough. Furthermore, such systems generate high volumes of false positives, leading to customer dissatisfaction and increased operational costs. The evolution of fraud detection into predictive science marks a pivotal transition, one where intelligent model can learn from historical data, uncover complex patterns, and anticipate fraudulent activity in real time.

At the heart of predictive fraud detection lies the ability to identify anomalies within transactional or behavioral data. However, unlike generic anomaly detection, fraud prediction requires the distinction between anomalies that are malicious and those that are benign but rare. A genuine high-value purchase may look anomalous based on prior behavior, but it is not necessarily fraudulent. Therefore, predictive models must achieve a delicate balance between sensitivity (catching fraud) and specificity (avoiding false alarms). This calls for a deep understanding of data relationships, temporal dynamics, and contextual information.

The deployment of predictive fraud detection systems begins with data. In domains such as finance, telecommunications, e-commerce, and insurance, systems collect a wide range of features, including transaction amount, frequency, geolocation, device metadata, and customer profile information. This data is then processed to extract meaningful signals, often through feature engineering. For example, a model might calculate how frequently a user makes international transactions, how often purchases are made late at night, or how the average transaction size has shifted over time. These behavioral indicators form the input for the model's predictive engine.

Early implementations of predictive fraud detection made use of supervised learning models such as logistic regression, decision trees, and support vector machines. These models are trained on labeled datasets where historical transactions are annotated as either fraudulent or legitimate. Over time, the model learns to associate certain patterns with fraud and makes predictions on new, unseen data. While interpretable and relatively fast to train, these models are limited in their ability to capture non-linear relationships and interactions among features, limitations that become pronounced in high-dimensional datasets.

To address this, ensemble methods such as random forests and gradient boosting machines became popular. These models aggregate the predictions of multiple weak learners to improve overall performance. In fraud detection, where individual signals may be weak or ambiguous, ensemble methods can leverage the collective intelligence of multiple trees to enhance accuracy. They are particularly adept at handling feature interactions and are more robust to overfitting compared to single decision trees.

However, the most significant breakthroughs in recent years have come from deep learning. With the ability to model complex and hierarchical representations, deep neural networks can uncover subtle patterns that traditional models may miss. For example, a recurrent neural network (RNN) can analyze the sequence of transactions over time to determine if the current behavior deviates from an individual's historical norm. A sudden change in transaction frequency or location, when seen in isolation, may not seem suspicious. But when contextualized within a timeline, it may represent a red flag. Long Short-Term Memory (LSTM) networks, a specialized form of RNNs, have proven particularly effective in this context due to their ability to retain long-term dependencies in time-series data.

In parallel, autoencoders unsupervised neural networks trained to reconstruct input data have gained traction in fraud detection. These models learn to compress normal transaction patterns and reconstruct them with high fidelity. When a transaction deviates significantly from the learned normal, the reconstruction error increases, signaling a potential anomaly. Unlike supervised models, which rely on labeled data, autoencoders can function even in scenarios where fraud examples are scarce or evolving.

Yet, the practical deployment of predictive models for fraud detection involves more than just model accuracy. One of the biggest challenges faced by organizations is the issue of data imbalance. Fraudulent transactions represent a tiny fraction of overall activity, sometimes as little as 0.1 percent. This imbalance can lead to models that are biased toward predicting the majority class, thereby missing fraud. Techniques such as resampling, cost-sensitive learning, and the use of synthetic data generation (like SMOTE—Synthetic Minority Over-sampling Technique) are used to mitigate this problem. However, even with these strategies, achieving a high recall without compromising precision remains a balancing act.

In addition to imbalance, concept drift is another persistent challenge. Fraudsters continuously adapt their tactics, and models trained on historical data may become obsolete. For example, during the COVID-19 pandemic, consumer behavior changed drastically, and fraud patterns shifted accordingly. This meant that models had to be retrained more frequently, and monitoring systems had to be adapted in near real-time. This dynamic nature of fraud necessitates a continuous learning framework where models are updated, validated, and redeployed in a timely manner. Some systems employ online learning, where the model updates itself incrementally as new data arrives. Others rely on periodic retraining based on drift detection metrics.

A further consideration is explainability. In domains where decisions directly affect individuals such as freezing a bank account or denying a loan, transparency becomes essential. Deep learning models, while accurate, are often considered "black boxes." This can pose problems for compliance, particularly in regulated industries. Techniques such as LIME (Local Interpretable Model-Agnostic Explanations) and SHAP (SHapley

Additive exPlanations) provide post-hoc interpretability by attributing predictions to individual features. These tools help analysts understand why a transaction was flagged, enabling better validation and informed intervention.

My own journey in building predictive fraud detection systems has involved close collaboration between data scientists, security analysts, and system architects. One key lesson is that fraud prediction is not solely a technical problem, it is a socio-technical one. The effectiveness of a model depends not just on its algorithmic performance but also on how well it integrates with human workflows, organizational risk appetite, and customer experience. For instance, a model that generates too many false positives may overwhelm fraud analysts and erode trust in the system. Conversely, a model that is too lenient may miss critical threats. The solution lies in developing a feedback loop where flagged transactions are reviewed, outcomes are logged, and the model is continuously refined based on operational insights.

Moreover, fraud detection must be embedded in a broader ecosystem of risk management. Predictive models work best when complemented by other security measures such as behavioral biometrics, device fingerprinting, and multi-factor authentication. For example, a financial platform may combine transaction analysis with device reputation scoring to determine whether to block, allow, or step up authentication for a given user. This layered defense strategy reduces dependency on any single model and increases overall system resilience.

The ethical dimension of predictive fraud detection cannot be overlooked. As systems become more autonomous, the risk of biased or discriminatory outcomes increases. Historical data may contain biases such as disproportionate scrutiny of certain demographic groups, and these can be inadvertently learned and perpetuated by models. Responsible AI practices require that models be audited for fairness, transparency, and accountability. Additionally, customers must be informed when automated systems are involved in decision-making, and mechanisms should be in place to contest or appeal incorrect classifications.

In conclusion, predictive models for fraud detection represent one of the most critical innovations in securing intelligent infrastructure. By transitioning from reactive to proactive defense, these models enable organizations to stay one step ahead of increasingly agile and resourceful adversaries. Through the application of machine learning, deep learning, and continuous monitoring, it is possible to build fraud detection systems that are not only accurate and scalable but also ethical and explainable. The path forward involves embracing hybrid approaches, investing in adaptive learning frameworks, and fostering collaboration between technology and human expertise. In an age where data is both an asset and a liability, predictive fraud detection stands as a pillar of trust and resilience in digital systems.

As intelligent infrastructure continues to evolve, the security paradigms that govern how users and devices access systems must adapt to meet new challenges. In traditional computing environments, access control was relatively straightforward: users operated within fixed locations and devices, and systems were protected by perimeter-based security mechanisms. However, in modern intelligent systems characterized by distributed architecture, real-time data exchange, and heterogeneity of users and devices, these legacy access control models are no longer sufficient. The question is no longer merely who is accessing a system, but also from where, when, using what device, and under what contextual conditions. To secure intelligent systems in such dynamic environments, there is an urgent need to reinvent access control architectures in ways that are adaptive, context-aware, and resilient.

Access control, at its core, is the mechanism by which a system determines whether a subject (such as a user, device, or process) has permission to perform a specific action on a resource. Traditionally, access control models have followed static principles. Role-Based Access Control (RBAC), for instance, assigns permissions to roles rather than individuals. While RBAC introduced scalability and manageability, it still assumes a relatively static environment where roles and privileges are predefined and unchanging. In intelligent infrastructure, this assumption breaks down. A sensor node in a smart grid might change its operating state multiple times in a day. A healthcare worker may require temporary access to a patient's record during an emergency, even if their default role does not permit it. These scenarios demand a more dynamic and responsive access control framework.

One of the most significant developments in this space has been the adoption of Attribute-Based Access Control (ABAC), where decisions are made based on attributes of the user, resource, action, and environment. ABAC allows fine-grained access decisions that take into account the specific context of a request. For example, access may be granted if the user is a certified physician, accessing the record from within the hospital network, during working hours. This level of granularity is well-suited for intelligent environments where static policies cannot capture the complexity of interactions. However, implementing ABAC at scale presents challenges related to policy management, attribute collection, and performance overhead. In highly dynamic systems, ensuring that policies remain consistent, updated, and enforced in real-time becomes an operational burden.

To further modernize access control, many organizations and system architects have turned to the concept of Zero Trust Architecture (ZTA). Zero Trust operates on the principle that no user or device, whether inside or outside the network, should be automatically trusted. Instead, verification is required for every access attempt, regardless of location or role. Zero Trust represents a philosophical shift from perimeter-based security to identity-centric security. In practice, this means continuously validating credentials, monitoring behavior, and adapting access rights based on real-time risk assessment.

In my experience working with intelligent infrastructure across sectors, Zero Trust has proven to be particularly relevant in environments where remote access, multi-device usage, and hybrid cloud deployments are prevalent. For instance, in a smart city infrastructure where traffic management systems, surveillance networks, and emergency response platforms are interconnected, a breach in one system could cascade into others. Implementing Zero Trust ensures that even if one node is compromised, lateral movement is restricted through continuous authentication and micro-segmentation. However, successful deployment of ZTA requires more than technology. It involves organizational change, including rethinking identity governance, enforcing the least privilege principles, and integrating analytics for behavior-based decision-making.

Another transformative approach to access control in dynamic environments involves the use of adaptive authentication. Rather than treating all login attempts equally, adaptive systems assess risk dynamically and adjust the authentication process accordingly. A user logging in from their usual location and device may pass with a single factor, such as a password. The same user attempting access from an unfamiliar location or device might be required to provide additional verification, such as a biometric scan or one-time passcode. Adaptive authentication blends user experience with security, ensuring that access is both frictionless and risk sensitive. In intelligent systems where users frequently switch contexts such as mobile workers, IoT devices, or remote healthcare teams, this flexibility becomes a necessity.

While adaptive authentication improves real-time decision-making, it also raises critical concerns about privacy, data collection, and fairness. Gathering contextual information such as geolocation, device identifiers, or behavioral biometrics can be intrusive if not managed properly. Users must be informed about what data is being collected and how it is used. Consent, transparency, and accountability are essential in building trust. Furthermore, access control models must be evaluated for bias. For example, reliance on behavioral biometrics could inadvertently disadvantage users with disabilities or those using assistive technologies. As systems grow more intelligent, access decisions increasingly rely on opaque algorithms, making it difficult to explain why access was denied or granted. This lack of transparency can erode confidence in the system and may also run afoul of regulatory requirements.

To address these issues, explainable access control models are gaining traction. These models incorporate mechanisms that allow users and administrators to understand the reasoning behind access decisions. Techniques such as rule tracing, visual policy editors, and natural language explanations are being developed to make access control policies more understandable. In regulated sectors like healthcare and finance, where access decisions must be auditable, explainable models not only enhance transparency but also facilitate compliance with standards such as HIPAA, GDPR, and ISO 27001.

Another dimension of reinventing access control involves managing machine-to-machine interactions. In intelligent infrastructure, not all subjects are human. Devices, applications, and autonomous agents often need to access data, issue commands, or perform automated actions. For example, a smart irrigation controller in agriculture may need to access weather data, sensor inputs, and control valves based on predictive analytics. Traditional identity and access management systems are not well-suited to managing the identities of thousands of non-human actors. This challenge is compounded by device churn, firmware updates, and intermittent connectivity. Solutions such as decentralized identity frameworks, digital certificates, and mutual authentication protocols are being explored to provide scalable and secure access control for non-human entities. The rise of blockchain-based access control models, which use distributed ledgers to record and verify permissions, also holds promise for decentralized environments.

Yet even the most advanced access control mechanisms are only as effective as their integration with real-time monitoring and response capabilities. Intelligent systems must not only grant access based on current context but also monitor what users and devices do after access is granted. Behavioral analytics, session monitoring, and post-access audits are essential components of a holistic access control strategy. An employee who receives legitimate access to a file system may still engage in data exfiltration or misuse of privileges. Therefore, systems must combine access decisions with runtime enforcement and anomaly detection. Integration between access control systems and security information and event management (SIEM) tools enables timely detection of policy violations and automated response.

One of the most promising areas in this field is the use of artificial intelligence to dynamically generate and enforce access control policies. Policy mining techniques use historical access logs to infer usage patterns and suggest optimal policies. Machine learning models can detect access anomalies, recommend changes to permissions, and even auto-adjust access rights based on behavioral trends. For example, if a user consistently accesses only a subset of their assigned resources, the system may recommend revoking unnecessary privileges to enforce the principle of least privilege. However, care must be taken to ensure that automated policy adjustments do not inadvertently lock out users or introduce operational bottlenecks. Human oversight remains critical, especially in high-stakes environments.

Reinventing access control in dynamic environments is not merely a technical endeavor; it is also a strategic one. Organizations must align their access control strategies with broader goals of digital transformation, user experience, and regulatory compliance. Governance structures must be established to define who sets policies, how they are updated, and how conflicts are resolved. Training and awareness are equally important. Users need to understand not just how to access systems securely but also why certain controls are in place. In the absence of such understanding, users may attempt to bypass controls, leading to shadow IT practices and increased risk exposure.

In conclusion, the reinvention of access control is essential to the security and resilience of intelligent infrastructure. Static models rooted in past paradigms are ill-equipped to handle the complexity, fluidity, and diversity of modern systems. By embracing adaptive, context-aware, and intelligent access control mechanisms, organizations can strike a balance between security and usability. Zero Trust principles, attribute-based decision-making, machine learning-driven policies, and explainability together form the foundation of next-generation access control. As we continue to embed intelligence into our critical systems from cities and energy grids to hospitals and manufacturing plants, the ability to manage access dynamically and responsibly will define the security posture of the future. My work in this space is driven by the belief that secure access is not a constraint but an enabler empowering users, protecting assets, and building trust in an increasingly connected world.

The promise of intelligent infrastructure is immense, offering transformative potential across sectors such as energy, transportation, healthcare, and urban planning. However, this promise does not come without substantial risks. As these systems grow more autonomous and interconnected, they are increasingly deployed in contexts marked by volatility be it political instability, economic uncertainty, natural disasters, cyber warfare, or rapidly shifting technological landscapes. Securing intelligent systems in such volatile contexts requires more than conventional security practices; it demands foresight, adaptability, resilience, and a deep understanding of both human and technical dimensions of risk.

Volatile environments are, by nature, unpredictable. In regions experiencing political unrest, for example, critical infrastructure such as power grids, communication systems, and transportation networks may become targets of sabotage, espionage, or unauthorized control. Similarly, in the aftermath of natural disasters like floods, wildfires, or earthquakes, smart infrastructure may become compromised not only physically but also in terms of data integrity and operational continuity. Economic instability can also disrupt the funding and maintenance of intelligent systems, leaving them exposed to obsolescence and unpatched vulnerabilities. In such high-risk settings, the security of intelligent systems must be reimagined from the ground up to account for both intentional threats and systemic fragility.

A fundamental principle in securing intelligent systems under volatile conditions is the design of resilience into the architecture. Resilience refers to the ability of a system to maintain its core functionality in the face of disruption, adapt to changing conditions, and recover quickly from incidents. This extends beyond redundancy or backup systems; it involves embedding adaptive intelligence into the very fabric of the infrastructure. For instance, in a smart transportation network operating in a region prone to civil unrest, it is not enough to encrypt traffic signals or monitor surveillance feeds. The system must be capable of autonomous rerouting, dynamic threat assessment, and localized decision-making even when central command structures are inaccessible. This level of autonomy requires advanced machine learning, decentralized computing, and real-time analytics.

Decentralization plays a critical role in enhancing the resilience of intelligent systems. In volatile contexts where central systems may be vulnerable to attack or failure, distributing computation and control can prevent single points of failure. Technologies such as edge computing and blockchain offer powerful tools for decentralization. Edge computing allows data processing to occur closer to the source at the device or sensor level thereby reducing dependency on centralized servers and improving real-time response. Blockchain, on the other hand, enables distributed consensus and immutable record-keeping, which can help verify transactions, authenticate users, and secure communications even in environments where trust is low or compromised.

However, decentralization also introduces new challenges, particularly in terms of coordination, latency, and policy enforcement. In decentralized systems, security policies must be replicated and enforced uniformly across diverse nodes, each of which may have differing computational capabilities and levels of trust. Ensuring consistency and synchronization in such a setting requires sophisticated consensus mechanisms and security protocols tailored to resource-constrained environments. Moreover, the potential for local compromise where one node behaves maliciously necessitates robust anomaly detection, authentication, and sandboxing techniques to prevent system-wide contamination.

Another layer of complexity arises from the human factor. In volatile contexts, human behavior becomes harder to predict and more difficult to manage. Misinformation, panic, and distrust can exacerbate technical vulnerabilities. For instance, during a geopolitical crisis, actors may disseminate fake alerts through compromised intelligent systems, causing chaos and undermining public confidence. In such scenarios, cybersecurity must intersect with information integrity and psychological safety. Designing systems that not only resist manipulation but also provide verifiable and transparent communication becomes essential. Cryptographically signed messages, multi-channel alerts, and clear user interfaces are critical to ensuring that intelligent systems remain credible sources of truth during uncertainty.

My work in deploying intelligent infrastructure in regions marked by social or economic instability has underscored the value of ethical hacking and red teaming. Ethical hacking involves proactively probing a system for weaknesses before adversaries can exploit them. Red teams simulate real-world attack scenarios, testing not only technical defenses but also the decision-making and response capabilities of the system's operators. These exercises reveal both technical gaps and organizational blind spots. For instance, a red team may discover that although an access control system is technically sound, poor configuration practices and inadequate training among staff render it vulnerable. In volatile environments, where real-world adversaries may be highly motivated and resourceful, such simulations provide invaluable insights.

Hardening the system, making it more resistant to attack is another cornerstone of securing intelligent infrastructure. This involves minimizing the system's attack surface by disabling unnecessary services, closing unused ports, and removing redundant code. It also includes regular patching of known vulnerabilities, even in constrained or isolated environments. However, in volatile settings, access to updates or vendor support may be disrupted. Therefore, systems must be designed to function securely even when isolated from the internet or external update services. Local patch repositories, digital signatures for offline verification, and fallback configurations can help maintain integrity in such conditions.

A proactive approach to security also necessitates the integration of predictive analytics. Rather than relying solely on retrospective detection of incidents, predictive models can assess environmental, behavioral, and operational indicators to forecast potential risks. For example, a smart building system might detect increasing power fluctuations, rising ambient temperature, and anomalous network traffic all of which, when combined, signal a probable coordinated attack or system failure. These insights, derived from data fusion and machine learning, enable preemptive action such as isolating components, throttling operations, or alerting human operators before damage occurs. However, predictive systems must be carefully calibrated to minimize false positives, especially in high-stakes environments where overreaction can be as disruptive as inaction.

Resilience also depends on the ability to restore systems quickly after disruption. This includes both technical recovery such as data restoration and reinitialization of services and operational continuity. Intelligent infrastructure must be designed with robust backup strategies, failover mechanisms, and continuity plans that reflect the realities of volatile environments. For instance, in a smart health clinic operating in a conflict zone, backups must not only be offsite but also physically secure and portable. Systems should support rapid reconfiguration and redeployment, possibly through containerization or lightweight virtualization technologies. Furthermore, documentation, training, and drills must be regularly updated and rehearsed to ensure that personnel are capable of executing recovery procedures under pressure.

The ethics of securing intelligent systems in volatile contexts also demand careful consideration. There is often a temptation, especially by powerful stakeholders or governments, to use intelligent infrastructure for surveillance, coercion, or political manipulation under the guise of security. The line between securing a system and using it for control can blur quickly in fragile contexts. To maintain legitimacy and protect human rights, security measures must be transparent, proportionate, and subject to oversight. Privacy-preserving technologies such as differential privacy, federated learning, and encrypted computation can help reconcile security objectives with civil liberties. Governance frameworks must include representation from affected communities and provide avenues for redress in case of abuse.

In one of my recent engagements involving a smart agriculture network in a region with volatile weather and unstable governance, we faced the challenge of ensuring data integrity and operational continuity despite frequent internet outages and cyber threats from politically motivated actors. Our solution involved deploying a mesh network of IoT sensors that communicated locally through Bluetooth Low Energy and Wi-Fi Direct protocols. Each node was equipped with basic anomaly detection capabilities and could operate autonomously if disconnected from the central controller. Data was logged locally and then synchronized with the central system whenever connectivity was restored. Critical data such as irrigation schedules and soil health metrics were cryptographically signed to prevent tampering. The system's resilience was further bolstered by a local web interface that allowed farmers to monitor and adjust settings even in the absence of internet access. This deployment illustrated that with the right architectural principles, even small-scale intelligent systems can be made robust against the shocks of a volatile environment.

Looking ahead, the security of intelligent systems in volatile contexts must evolve in tandem with the threats they face. This evolution includes the integration of artificial general intelligence (AGI) capabilities that can autonomously adapt security strategies, self-heal after breaches, and collaborate with human operators in a symbiotic fashion. However, the move toward AGI also raises new questions about accountability, control, and unintended consequences. Who is responsible when an autonomous system takes a security action that causes collateral damage? How do we ensure that intelligent systems do not inherit the biases or blind spots of their creators? Addressing these questions requires interdisciplinary collaboration, rigorous testing, and inclusive governance.

Securing intelligent systems in volatile contexts is one of the most complex challenges in modern cybersecurity. It demands a paradigm shift from perimeter defenses to adaptive, resilient, and ethically grounded systems. By embracing decentralization, predictive analytics, ethical hacking, and human-centered design, we can build intelligent infrastructure that not only withstands the turbulence of unstable environments but actively contributes to their stabilization. Security, in this context, is not merely the absence of threats, it is the presence of trust, continuity, and the capacity to adapt and recover. My work in this domain continues to be driven by a simple but profound belief: that the true measure of a security system is not how it performs in calm waters, but how it endures and evolves in the storm.

CHAPTER 7

T he most sophisticated machine learning models, no matter how accurate or mathematically elegant, have little value unless their outputs lead to informed action. For I, the true measure of a data model is not the complexity of its architecture or the novelty of its technique, but its capacity to drive meaningful and measurable change in a business context. In an era where organizations are flooded with data but often starved of clarity, the role of a data scientist extends beyond coding and computation, it requires strategic translation. It is in this space between technical insight and practical application that I have built a reputation, consistently ensuring that data products become engines of decision-making, not just artifacts of analysis.

Translating model outcomes into business strategy begins with an awareness of who the model is serving. While the technical metrics such as precision, recall, or F1-score are indispensable for internal evaluation, they are often meaningless to business stakeholders. A 92% accuracy score means little to a product manager unless it can be linked directly to customer satisfaction, retention, or revenue. Its approach is to serve as a bridge, not just between data and business, but between statistical evidence and strategic intuition. This bridging role requires fluency in both domains: an understanding of how models behave under various conditions, and a grasp of what levers matter most in business decision-making.

One of my core principles is that data science must begin and end with a business question. Before a single line of code is written, he insists on working with stakeholders to define the decisions the model is expected to inform. Is the goal to prioritize sales leads? To reduce churn? To identify inefficiencies in supply chain logistics? By framing the problem as a decision rather than a dataset, I ensure that the modeling process is embedded in a cycle of action. This upfront clarity also guards against the all-too-common pitfall of building technically robust models that solve the wrong problem or that optimize metrics with no strategic relevance.

Once the model is developed, I turn my attention to interpretability. Contrary to the belief that business leaders are disinterested in the technical workings of models, I have found that trust and adoption increase dramatically when stakeholders understand why a model behaves the way it does. He makes deliberate efforts to explain key drivers of the model's predictions whether through SHAP values, partial dependence plots, or simplified rule-based approximations. These techniques allow stakeholders to see which features are influencing outcomes, how changes in input variables affect predictions, and where uncertainty lies. For me, interpretability is not about simplifying the science; it is about empowering decision-makers with confidence and insight.

However, interpretability is not sufficient on its own. A model may be explainable yet still fail to influence strategy if it is not integrated into the business workflow. I ensure that model outputs are not left in a dashboard but are delivered directly into the systems where decisions are made whether that means feeding propensity scores into a CRM platform, pushing fraud flags into transaction systems, or delivering dynamic pricing suggestions into an e-commerce engine. Integration is the litmus test for impact. Without it, models remain passive tools; with it, they become active collaborators in the business process.

Another area where I excel is in scenario planning. He recognizes that in volatile or uncertain environments, decision-makers are less interested in point predictions and more concerned with ranges, probabilities, and trade-offs. In one project involving demand forecasting for a retail chain, I presented not just a single forecast, but three conditional scenarios: one based on conservative assumptions, one on aggressive growth, and one on historical trends. Each scenario was accompanied by a confidence interval and a business narrative explaining the underlying assumptions. This allowed executives to prepare contingency plans and allocate resources flexibly rather than anchoring on a single figure. By contextualizing model outputs within a spectrum of possible futures, I equip leaders to make robust, not just reactive, decisions.

In some cases, the process of translating insight into impact also requires reframing the model's narrative. For example, in a customer retention project, the model I built predicted churn with over 85% accuracy. However, early feedback from the marketing team revealed that the term "churn probability" triggered defensive thinking and reactive planning. By reframing the same output as "retention opportunity score," I shifted the conversation from risk avoidance to proactive engagement. The model's effect was the same, but its perception changed and with it, the energy and alignment of the team. This is a subtle but critical lesson in stakeholder psychology: language shapes response, and model adoption often hinges as much on framing as on performance.

I also recognize that translating model outcomes into strategy involves negotiating trade-offs. Models often reveal tensions between competing objectives such as maximizing short-term revenue versus long-term customer loyalty or minimizing fraud versus maintaining user experience. Rather than presenting model results as definitive truths, I use them to inform deliberation. He sets up decision frameworks that clarify the costs and benefits of different actions, helping stakeholders see how changing thresholds or weights affects outcomes. This decision-theoretic approach reinforces the idea that models do not replace judgment, they refine it.

In several instances, the impact has been felt most strongly not through the immediate deployment of a model, but through the organizational learning it stimulates. In one case, a segmentation model revealed that a particular demographic previously considered low value actually had high engagement and lifetime value when reached through specific channels. This insight challenged longstanding assumptions in the marketing strategy. Though it took months for the campaign to be redesigned, the shift in perception catalyzed a broader cultural change: teams began to question their priors and lean more heavily on data to challenge intuition. In this way, I's models act as catalysts for epistemic humility and organizational agility.

I also emphasize the importance of monitoring and iteration. Once a model is deployed, its performance must be tracked not just through technical metrics but through business KPIs. I design feedback loops where business impact such as changes in conversion rate, fraud loss, or customer lifetime value is linked back to the model's recommendations. If the model does not move the needle on these outcomes, it must be retrained, recalibrated, or retired. This lifecycle mindset ensures that models do not become obsolete or counterproductive over time. It also reinforces accountability: if a model is used to make a decision, then the decision's results should inform the next version of the model.

Finally, I am mindful of the ethical and reputational dimensions of model deployment. In sectors such as finance, healthcare, or education, the consequences of model-driven decisions can be profound. A loan denied, a diagnosis delayed, a student miscategorized each has a human cost. It incorporates fairness and risk assessment into the translation process, ensuring that models are not only technically sound but socially responsible. He conducts bias audits, stress-tests scenarios for disparate impact, and works with legal and compliance teams to anticipate potential harms. For me, the strategic impact of a model cannot be separated from its ethical footprint.

Translating model outcomes into strategic decisions is neither a technical afterthought nor a mere communication exercise. It is a complex, iterative process that demands technical acumen, business fluency, and emotional intelligence. Its ability to move seamlessly between code and conversation, between insight and action, is what distinguishes his work. He does not merely build models, he builds momentum. By anchoring data science in business reality, reframing outputs in actionable terms, and embedding models into operational systems, I ensure that insight does not remain theoretical but becomes a driving force for strategic decision-making. In an age where data is abundant, but clarity is scarce, his work reminds us that the ultimate purpose of a model is not just to predict the future, but to help shape it.

In today's business landscape, the most impactful data science work does not happen in isolation. It is not confined to a silo of analysts poring over data sets in solitude. Instead, it lives at the intersection of departments, disciplines, and domains. For me, the power of a model is magnified when it is developed not as a technical artifact, but as a collaborative product of shared insight and mutual goals. His experience across diverse industries has shown again and again that the success of any data initiative rests less on the complexity of the algorithm and more on the quality of collaboration that supports it. In his approach, cross-functional collaboration is not a convenience, it is the foundation.

The process of building and deploying a successful data product often involves a constellation of stakeholders: product managers, engineers, marketers, operations teams, legal advisors, and executives. Each of these roles brings unique perspectives, priorities, and constraints to the table. A product manager might be focused on user retention, an engineer might be concerned with scalability and performance, and a legal team might be focused on compliance and data ethics. The strength lies in his ability to navigate these varying interests without compromising the technical integrity of the model or the strategic intent of the business.

He begins every major data initiative by convening the right voices early in the process. Rather than waiting until the model is built to involve business stakeholders, I pull them into the room from day one. This early collaboration serves multiple purposes: it clarifies objectives, identifies constraints, and builds ownership. More importantly, it surfaces implicit assumptions that might otherwise derail the project later. For instance, in a fraud detection system built for a financial service provider, the operations team initially expected real-time flags, while the engineers had planned for a batch-processing architecture. By initiating cross-functional alignment upfront, I was able to set realistic expectations, co-create priorities, and avoid last-minute rework.

Communication plays a central role in a collaborative method. He does not assume that business teams speak the language of data science, nor does he water down his insights to the point of meaninglessness. Instead, he translates technical findings into stories, analogies, and frameworks that resonate with each audience. When discussing a clustering algorithm with marketing stakeholders, he might describe customer groups as behavioral "tribes" with distinct habits, affinities, and triggers. With engineers, he may focus on the data schema, latency trade-offs, and system load. This flexible communication style not only demystifies the model's logic but also builds rapport and trust.

Trust, indeed, is the currency of effective cross-functional work. I have found that stakeholders are more willing to act on model outputs when they understand the process, see their feedback incorporated, and feel that their domain expertise is valued. This is especially important in organizations where data science is a newer discipline and skepticism lingers. In one instance, while working with a sales team on a lead scoring system, I made it a point to involve sales representatives in the feature selection process. Their knowledge of customer behavior led to the inclusion of nuanced variables such as frequency of returned calls and lead source credibility that significantly improved the model's accuracy. But more importantly, their involvement transformed their relationship with the model: they no longer saw it as a black box imposed by "the data guys," but as a tool they had helped to shape.

Conflict, of course, is inevitable in any cross-functional collaboration. Misaligned incentives, competing deadlines, and resource constraints can strain even the most well-intentioned teams. I approached these tensions not as roadblocks, but as signals. A disagreement between the legal team and product managers about user tracking policies may indicate a deeper uncertainty about data governance. A clash between engineering and data science over architecture may reveal a need for better system documentation. Rather than circumvent these conflicts, I facilitate structured conversations to surface root causes, find common ground, and co-create solutions. My experience has taught me that the goal is not consensus for its own sake, but alignment on principles, priorities, and trade-offs.

One of the most innovative aspects of this collaborative style is his use of "data co-design" sessions. In these workshops, he invites stakeholders from different departments to collaboratively sketch out what the model should look like not just in terms of features and outcomes, but in terms of how it will live within the business ecosystem. These sessions often include whiteboarding exercises, persona mapping, journey modeling, and mock dashboards. The process creates a shared mental model of how data will flow, how decisions will be made, and what success will look like. It also uncovers potential pitfalls such as ethical concerns, data quality issues, or operational bottlenecks before they become crises.

I also champion a product management mindset within data teams. He encourages his colleagues to think not just about building models but about delivering value. This means defining success metrics that reflect business outcomes, establishing feedback loops, and continuously iterating based on user feedback. By adopting the rhythms and rituals of product development such as agile sprints, user stories, and retrospectives, he brings data teams closer to the cadence of the broader organization. This integration enhances not only collaboration, but also relevance: the models being built are more likely to be adopted, monitored, and improved.

Crucially, I do not see collaboration as a one-time event but as an ongoing relationship. Once a model is deployed, he continues to engage with stakeholders to track its performance, gather feedback, and refine its functionality. I hold regular review sessions to assess whether the model meets expectations, how user behavior is evolving, and whether new data or requirements warrant retraining. In one campaign optimization project, weekly check-ins with the marketing team revealed a seasonal shift in consumer behavior that was not yet reflected in the data. By responding quickly, I avoided a significant performance drop and demonstrated the value of continuous cross-functional vigilance.

Leadership plays a vital role in fostering this culture of collaboration. I actively mentor junior data scientists on how to engage with non-technical stakeholders, how to listen for business pain points, and how to frame data work in terms of customer impact. He also advocates for the inclusion of data roles in strategic planning forums, believing that when data professionals are invited into the room where decisions are made, their insights become more relevant, timely, and actionable. This proactive positioning of data science as a strategic partner not a service desk has transformed how his teams are perceived and how they operate.

In global organizations, cross-functional collaboration also includes bridging cultural and geographic differences. My work with distributed teams has taught me the importance of empathy, clarity, and patience. I tailor my communication to accommodate time zones, language barriers, and organizational hierarchies. I leverage collaboration tools not just to share information but to build community. In one multinational project involving teams in Lagos, Berlin, and Singapore, he coordinated asynchronous sprint planning, created video explainers for complex concepts, and established shared repositories for documentation. This attention to detail fostered cohesion across continents and demonstrated that collaboration is not merely about processes, it is about relationships.

In conclusion, collaboration across cross-functional teams is not a peripheral concern in data science; it is the engine that drives relevance, adoption, and impact. Its work illustrates that technical excellence must be paired with interpersonal fluency, organizational awareness, and a genuine respect for diverse expertise. By embedding collaboration into every stage of the model lifecycle from ideation to deployment to iteration, he ensures that data products do not sit idle in isolation but become integrated, living components of the business. His approach reminds us that data does not speak for itself, it speaks through the voices of the people who build it, question it, and act on it together.

In a world where data science is often evaluated by the elegance of its models or the complexity of its pipelines, it's easy to lose sight of the fundamental reason businesses invest in data science in the first place: to drive value. That value may take many forms, greater efficiency, stronger customer retention, higher revenue, better risk management but it must always be tangible and measurable. For I, the journey from algorithm to impact is incomplete unless the models he builds directly influence outcomes that matter to the organization. In his philosophy, data science is not just about what is statistically significant, but what is strategically significant.

The divide between technical metrics and business goals is one of the most persistent challenges in the field. Accuracy, precision, recall, and F1-scores are foundational to evaluating model performance from a statistical perspective. However, these metrics rarely capture the real-world impact of a model. A fraud detection system with a high precision rate might still miss high-value fraud if thresholds are misaligned. A churn prediction model with excellent recall might generate interventions that are too costly to justify. In other words, technical performance is necessary, but it is not sufficient. Its approach is to translate technical metrics into business-relevant language, reframing success in terms of customer outcomes, operational savings, or growth opportunities.

This alignment process begins at the model design stage. I insist on defining success collaboratively, with stakeholders from marketing, finance, operations, and customer service involved from the start. Instead of asking, "Can we predict X with high accuracy?" the framing becomes, "What would we do differently if we could predict X accurately?" This question shifts the conversation from performance to action. For example, in building a customer lifetime value (CLV) model for a subscription-based platform, the metric of interest was not simply the R^2 value of the regression but how effectively the model could identify high-value customers early enough for targeted engagement. The model's business utility came not from how well it fit historical data, but from how it influenced retention strategy and revenue forecasting.

To bridge the gap between data science and business outcomes, I often develop composite metrics that reflect both technical rigor and economic relevance. In a product recommendation system, for example, he might measure not just click-through rate (CTR) or top N accuracy, but revenue per recommendation and net uplift in conversion. These business-centric metrics compel the team to think beyond model performance and toward behavioral impact. A model that improves CTR by 5% but increases customer acquisition cost (CAC) by 20% is not a win. Conversely, a model with slightly lower precision that expands lifetime value by aligning better with user intent may deliver far greater strategic benefit.

Another key part of the method is the concept of *model-to-value traceability*. This means that every model should have a clear, documented pathway linking its outputs to key performance indicators (KPIs) the business cares about. Whether it's reducing refund fraud, increasing subscription renewals, or shortening time-to-resolution in support centers, there must be a causal or at least strongly correlative relationship between what the model does and how the business performs. This traceability not only ensures that data science is grounded in reality, but also makes it easier to justify investment, secure buy-in, and foster accountability.

Crucially, I understand that aligning metrics with business value also requires contextual awareness. The same metric can mean different things in different situations. Take the case of customer churn. A churn rate of 15% might be disastrous for a telecom company but entirely acceptable for a seasonal e-commerce platform. Similarly, an increase in average resolution time in a call center may look like a negative KPI until it's revealed that agents are spending more time resolving complex issues to first-contact satisfaction. These nuances highlight the danger of optimizing blindly for generic metrics. Its work emphasizes the need for localized, purpose-built evaluation frameworks that reflect the actual goals of the business environment in question.

One of the most overlooked factors in this alignment process is the time horizon. Many models produce short-term wins but fail to consider long-term implications. I am intentional about balancing short-term KPIs with long-term strategic goals. For example, in pricing optimization, it's possible to boost immediate sales by offering aggressive discounts. But if the model does not account for customer perception, brand equity, or long-term profit margins, it may erode value over time. In response, I build temporal models and long-horizon simulations that estimate downstream effects, enabling business leaders to make trade-offs between present gains and future resilience.

Monitoring plays a vital role in keeping data science aligned with business value. I establish performance dashboards that do more than track technical drift or statistical deviation, they monitor business impact in real time. In a supply chain optimization project, for instance, the models improved delivery route efficiency. But the true measure of success was captured through metrics like cost savings per mile, delivery time variance, and customer satisfaction post-delivery. These KPIs were continuously tracked, and model adjustments were made in response to fluctuations in external factors such as weather, fuel costs, and regional regulations. This adaptive monitoring ensures that models remain responsive not just to data changes, but to shifts in business reality.

In my experience, the ultimate test of whether metrics matter is whether they influence decision-making. I often ask, "What decisions will this metric inform? What action will be taken if it rises or falls?" If a metric cannot answer these questions, it is not actionable and thus, not valuable. In one fraud analytics engagement, the initial metric used was the number of suspicious transactions flagged per day. While informative, it led to alert fatigue and overwhelmed the investigation team. I replaced it with a metric that measured the proportion of investigated flags that led to confirmed fraud, a change that not only improved operational focus but also increased trust in the model's recommendations.

I also stress the importance of sharing successes in a language the business understands. When a model drives improvement, it is not enough to show a change in RMSE or AUC. I quantify outcomes in terms of profit retained, time saved, risk avoided, or customer loyalty increased. These narratives help elevate data science from a support function to a strategic partner. In organizations where such alignment becomes embedded, data science evolves from a curiosity into a core engine of competitive advantage.

At the same time, I am candid about the risks of misalignment. He has seen models fail not due to technical flaws but because they were evaluated against irrelevant or misinterpreted metrics. A predictive maintenance model deployed in a manufacturing firm was initially celebrated for reducing machine downtime. However, it also increased overall maintenance costs due to overly cautious alerts. Without a balanced metric that combined uptime with cost efficiency, the model skewed incentives and created operational strain. I intervened by developing a cost-adjusted risk index that better captured the business's dual goals of reliability and affordability. This experience reaffirmed his belief that metrics must be holistic and multi-dimensional, especially in complex environments.

As artificial intelligence becomes more pervasive, the temptation to focus on performance metrics at the expense of business value is likely to grow. I cautions against this trend. He believes that the future of data science lies not in maximizing technical purity but in cultivating strategic relevance. This requires humility, curiosity, and a willingness to revisit assumptions. It means asking hard questions about how success is defined, measured, and experienced by customers and stakeholders alike.

In conclusion, aligning data science with business value is both an art and a discipline. It involves translating complex metrics into meaningful outcomes, designing models that respond to real needs, and continuously refining success definitions in light of evolving goals. The approach is a masterclass in this balance. By embedding business metrics into the fabric of model development and deployment, he ensures that data science is not an abstract endeavor but a practical force for progress. This work reminds us that the most important metrics are not the ones that impress, but the ones that compel action and in doing so, deliver value where it matters most.

CHAPTER 8

E very seasoned data scientist knows that failure is not an anomaly, it is a companion. While success stories tend to dominate conference stages and case studies, the truth is that behind every high-impact model are a dozen that fell short. For me, failure is neither shameful nor avoidable. It is a rite of passage, a mirror, and sometimes even a guide. In this subsection, he reflects on the models that didn't work, the lessons they taught, and how these setbacks shaped his maturity as both a technologist and a strategist.

One of my earliest failures involved a predictive pricing model designed for a mid-sized logistics company seeking to optimize shipping rates in real time. The model, built with historical route data, seasonal demand variables, and competitor pricing trends, performed flawlessly in testing. It passed all cross-validation checks, held up under stress simulations, and delivered what looked like a statistically sound pricing strategy. However, within weeks of deployment, the business began to suffer losses. Delivery volumes dropped, and partner dissatisfaction grew. The problem, as I later diagnosed, was not the model's math, it was its detachment from operational reality. The model failed to account for human behavior: drivers who began avoiding routes with new lower rates, customers who interpreted sudden price fluctuations as instability, and internal staff who didn't understand the rationale behind pricing adjustments. The model optimized for revenue in theory, but eroded trust in practice. It was a powerful lesson in the limitations of isolated modeling: technical precision cannot compensate for lack of systemic empathy.

Another failure came during an ambitious attempt to predict student dropout rates at a tertiary education institution. The goal was to help the school intervene early with at-risk students. I and my team gathered a rich dataset, including attendance logs, assignment completion, learning platform engagement, and even sentiment analysis from discussion forums. The model achieved impressive accuracy on the test set, and initial feedback from academic advisors was enthusiastic. But within the first semester of use, anomalies emerged. Several high-performing students were flagged as "at risk," and some who eventually dropped out had not been identified at all. Digging into the issue, I realized that the data used for training lacked a key dimension: mental health and social factors. Students facing financial distress, emotional burnout, or family obligations often did not exhibit academic decline until it was too late for the model to catch. Furthermore, the engagement signals were misinterpreted, for instance, a student with minimal platform usage might have been excelling in offline study groups. The model had measured the observable, but not the meaningful. This taught me that success depends not just on having more data, but on having the right data.

Perhaps the most humbling failure came not from a poorly performing model, but from a misjudged stakeholder relationship. In a healthcare analytics project involving hospital readmission rates, I developed a model intended to identify patients at high risk of returning within 30 days. The model was technically sound and deployed successfully. However, it triggered a backlash from nursing staff, who felt the scores were being used to critique their work unfairly. The model had become a symbol of surveillance, not support. What I missed was the emotional context in which the model would be received. While he had optimized for predictive accuracy and interpretability, he had failed to design the rollout with empathy. There was no onboarding, no training, no space for dialogue. The model's deployment felt imposed, not collaborative. Eventually, it had to be paused while new change management processes were introduced. This failure reminded me that successful modeling is not just about what the system predicts, but how people experience those predictions.

Each of these failures revealed different weaknesses such as technical, contextual, relational but they shared a common thread: a gap between model logic and real-world complexity. In all three cases, my models were internally consistent and externally disconnected. They worked well in test environments but collapsed under the weight of human nuance, social dynamics, and environmental volatility. What makes these failures formative is not just that they occurred, but that I examined them ruthlessly and used them to rewire his approach.

From the logistics pricing model, I learned the necessity of stakeholder validation before deployment. Now, I include a "human behavior audit" in a project checklist, a structured review of how proposed model outputs might influence people across the ecosystem. He asks: Will this model trigger resistance? Could it be misunderstood? Does it require a shift in workflow that stakeholders are not prepared for? By embedding behavioral foresight into his process, I ensure that models land softly, not disruptively.

From the dropout prediction failure, I took away a deeper respect for data limitations. Data richness does not guarantee relevance. Today, I insisted on working with domain experts during feature selection, not just data engineers or analysts. I listen closely to teachers, counselors, front-line staff and people who live with the problem the model is trying to solve. Their lived experiences often highlight variables that data alone cannot capture. I also now champion qualitative proxies using available indicators to approximate hidden factors. For example, rather than waiting for mental health metrics (which may be unavailable), I use patterns like late-night logins or uncharacteristic engagement dips as proxy signals, always clearly flagging their limitations.

The healthcare model's failure reshaped how I managed model adoption. I no longer treat deployment as a technical milestone but as a cultural event. I even map out stakeholder journeys, host pre-launch workshops, and establish feedback channels that allow users to express concerns before they escalate into opposition. Most importantly, I collaborate with organizational change experts to ensure that models are introduced as tools of empowerment, not judgment. The goal is not just adoption, but ownership.

Interestingly, I also came to see that some failures are a function of timing. In several cases, my models were built correctly but the organization simply wasn't ready. Either the supporting infrastructure was immature, or the culture was resistant to data-driven decision-making. Rather than forcing implementation, I now use such situations as an opportunity for education. He pilots smaller versions of the model, showcases their potential in low-stakes settings, and lets interest grow organically. Failure, in these moments, becomes a form of seeding. The model may fail as a product but succeed as a conversation starter.

What makes my reflection on failure so compelling is that it is never merely technical or defensive. He does not retreat into blaming data, shifting responsibility, or citing external variables. Instead, he treats every failure as a hypothesis disproven, a blind spot revealed, a skill matured. His attitude is not that of someone who avoids failure, but of someone who cultivates a resilient relationship with it. In a profession where the cost of being wrong can be high, and the pressure to be right is constant, this posture is both rare and powerful.

In conclusion, the models that fail often teach the deepest lessons not only about data science, but about human systems, communication, and the nature of complexity. For I, each miss is a message, pointing toward a more holistic, thoughtful, and empathetic practice. He no longer asks only, "Did the model work?" but also, "Did it *work for the world it entered?*" That shift from predictive power to contextual fit is the hallmark of his evolving mastery. In failure, I find refinement. In setbacks, he discovers strategy. And in the quiet postmortem of a flawed launch, he listens for the insights that will shape his next, better success.

In the high-stakes world of data science, feedback can arrive like a jolt. Sometimes it comes in the form of a failed pilot. Sometimes it's an irritated email from a product lead, a confused customer's query, or a subtle dip in a business KPI that was supposed to rise. In many organizations, feedback is treated as an unwelcome audit, a judgment passed on what went wrong. But for me, feedback is neither a post-mortem nor a rebuke. It is a signal. A directional cue. A mirror that reflects where understanding was misaligned or where assumptions quietly failed. I do not see feedback as a consequence of error, but as a necessary nutrient in the process of refinement.

Over time, I have developed a disciplined, almost reverent relationship with feedback. It is not incidental to his work; it is integral. Whether it comes from users, stakeholders, performance dashboards, or internal team retrospectives, he treats it as data just as real and actionable as any numerical feature in a training set. This orientation allows me to maintain emotional distance from the sting of criticism and instead focus on what it reveals. In my words, "Feedback doesn't say something about my failure, it says something about what the system didn't understand, or what I didn't ask it to do well enough."

One of the reasons I thrive in feedback-rich environments is because I set them up deliberately. Before any model goes live, he ensures there is a structured feedback loop attached to it. These loops often include a combination of quantitative and qualitative inputs. On the quantitative side, he implements real-time monitoring dashboards to track model drift, false positives, business KPIs, and system latency. On the qualitative side, he initiates stakeholder check-ins, internal usage surveys, and model experience sessions where users can express how they interpret and react to the model's outputs. By gathering multiple forms of feedback, he gets a multi-dimensional view of model performance not just in code, but in context.

In one case, while working on a dynamic pricing engine for a retail client, the feedback I received had little to do with accuracy and everything to do with perception. Customers were confused and annoyed by rapidly fluctuating prices, interpreting them as inconsistency or manipulation rather than responsiveness. This wasn't a failure of prediction, it was a failure of user experience. I took this insight seriously and collaborated with the design team to introduce explanatory labels next to price changes, clarifying that adjustments were based on demand or inventory levels. Over time, transparency improved user trust and engagement. The technical model remained the same; what changed was the ecosystem around it. This experience reinforced I's view that feedback is often not about whether a model is "right," but whether it *makes sense* to those who use it.

I also recognize that some of the most valuable feedback comes from what isn't said from silence, avoidance, or disengagement. If a team stops using a dashboard, he doesn't wait for complaints. He initiates exploratory conversations to find out why. Was the interface confusing? Were the insights too late to be useful? Did the model contradict domain intuition too often? By proactively chasing unspoken feedback, I uncover friction that might otherwise fester into resistance or irrelevance.

I am also quick to distinguish between feedback and noise. Not all responses are created equal. Some reflect misunderstanding rather than flaws. Others may be rooted in resistance to change. I approach feedback analysis the same way he approaches data preprocessing, he cleans, classifies, and weighs it. He identifies feedback that stems from legitimate mismatches between design and reality and separates it from noise generated by outliers or edge cases. This nuanced treatment prevents overcorrection while still honoring valuable input.

Crucially, I build psychological safety around feedback within his teams. He fosters a culture where reporting failures or discomfort is not a risk but a responsibility. In team retrospectives, he encourages honest debriefs: What surprised us? What didn't go as expected? What did we assume that turned out false? These rituals don't just diagnose problems; they teach teams how to learn. By framing feedback as a mechanism for curiosity rather than critique, I transform it from a weapon into a workshop.

One of the most innovative aspects of his feedback practice is what he calls *expectation-mapping*. Before deployment, I facilitate workshops where stakeholders write down what they expect the model to do, how they think it will behave, and what success looks like in their domain. After deployment, these same stakeholders revisit their expectations and compare them with reality. This creates a natural moment for reflection and recalibration. It also uncovers implicit expectations that may never have been articulated, expectations the model could not have been built to meet, simply because no one voiced them.

Feedback is also a crucial input for the ethical review process. In one instance, a recruitment algorithm he helped develop began surfacing disproportionately fewer candidates from underrepresented backgrounds. Although the model was technically blind to race, the feedback from the recruiting team and community stakeholders indicated a bias embedded in proxy variables like university attended or years of experience. I immediately initiated a root-cause audit, revised the model's weighting strategy, and added checks for demographic fairness. The feedback didn't merely fix the model, it helped the organization confront structural assumptions and take a more just approach to hiring. In this case, feedback was not just a signal of technical failure; it was a signal of ethical misalignment.

Over the years, I have come to see that the way an organization responds to feedback often determines whether its data science efforts thrive or stagnate. Teams that avoid feedback loops, suppress negative results, or penalize course correction tend to build fragile models, technically impressive, but disconnected and brittle. Teams that embrace feedback, however inconvenient, become more adaptable, more informed, and ultimately more impactful. I ensure that his teams fall into the latter category. He rewards insight over infallibility, adjustment over perfection, and responsiveness over rigidity.

In reflecting on his own growth, I often credit feedback for the evolution of his thinking. It was feedback that pushed me from seeing models as endpoints to understanding them as ongoing hypotheses. It was feedback that taught me to build not just for performance, but for comprehension and trust. And it was feedback that helped me make the shift from being a solo contributor to becoming a collaborative strategist, capable of guiding others through the messiness of real-world implementation.

In conclusion, feedback is not the enemy of innovation, it is its engine. For me, feedback is not something to tolerate or survive; it is something to seek, to structure, and to study. It turns mistakes into mechanisms, confusion into clarity, and doubt into direction. In treating feedback as a signal rather than a setback, it shows us that failure is not the end of the story, it is often where the most important parts begin.

Innovation is rarely linear. It does not move neatly from idea to execution to success. More often, it lurches forward in fits and starts, doubling back on itself, shedding assumptions, gathering insight, and adapting to resistance. For I, this messy reality is not a sign of dysfunction, it is the very architecture of meaningful progress. At the heart of his data science practice lies a quiet but powerful principle: iteration. To iterate is to admit uncertainty, to honor change, and to build systems that are as dynamic as the environments they serve. It is through this loop of building, testing, failing, listening, and rebuilding that I sustains innovation, not as a burst of brilliance, but as a durable, resilient rhythm.

Iteration is more than a development tactic; it is a mindset. It begins with how I define the role of a model. He does not see models as final answers, but as evolving hypotheses. A model is not "finished" when it achieves a certain level of accuracy; it is only mature when it has proven its utility, withstood friction, adapted to real-world anomalies, and earned trust in context. This view frees his teams from the pressure to be perfect on the first attempt and instead encourages a cycle of continual refinement. It also creates space for creativity. When failure is not fatal but formative, teams are more willing to experiment, more open to feedback, and more committed to long-term excellence.

One way I operationalize iteration is through staged deployment. Rather than launching models at full scale, he introduces them incrementally first in shadow mode, where predictions are made but not acted on, then in limited environments, such as one business unit or a single customer segment. This allows his team to compare model predictions with human decisions, identify anomalies, and adjust configurations before exposing the system to a wider impact. Each deployment stage is a feedback loop unto itself, generating insights that inform the next version of the model. This stepwise approach not only reduces risk but also creates multiple opportunities for learning.

Monitoring plays a critical role in the iteration loop. I design performance dashboards that do more than display technical metrics, they serve as early warning systems. He tracks leading indicators of failure such as user disengagement, decision reversals, unexplained outliers, and shifts in input data distributions. These dashboards are not static; they evolve alongside the model. As new variables are introduced or business priorities shift, the monitoring framework is updated to reflect what success now means. In I's ecosystem, no model is ever deployed without a plan for what happens next, and next again.

Version control, too, is part of the loop. I insist on rigorous model versioning not just to manage technical updates, but to support interpretability and accountability. Each version is documented with its assumptions, feature sets, performance benchmarks, and contextual notes about deployment conditions. This archival discipline means that when models are revisited months later, teams can trace the full history of their evolution. It also empowers retrospective analysis: why did version 3 perform better in Region A but worse in Region B? What business conditions were in play? Iteration is not just about looking forward, it's about remembering what worked and why.

The iteration loop is especially valuable in volatile or fast-moving environments. I's work in sectors like e-commerce, fintech, and logistics has shown me that static models decay quickly. Customer behavior evolves, markets fluctuate, regulations change, and data pipelines drift. In these settings, the ability to update a model frequently is not a luxury, it is a competitive necessity. My teams build infrastructure that supports rapid retraining, automated testing, and scheduled reevaluation. This agility allows the model to remain relevant, not just accurate. It also ensures that decisions based on those models are made with the freshest possible understanding of the world.

Yet iteration is not merely technical. I embeds it into team culture. In project retrospectives, he encourages open reflection on what surprised the team, what broke down, and what needs to change. These are not blame sessions, they are design sessions. They reframe frustration as fuel and discomfort as direction. He has found that when iteration is normalized, people become more honest, more collaborative, and more imaginative. They don't defend a model out of pride; they interrogate it out of purpose.

One of the deeper outcomes of this iterative philosophy is resilience not just in code, but in mindset. I train his teams to expect setbacks and to respond not with defensiveness but with design. In one project involving user personalization for a mobile banking app, the first model failed to increase engagement. Instead of rushing to tweak the algorithm, I paused the project and convened a cross-functional review. They discovered that users didn't trust the recommendations because they felt too generic, even though they were technically optimized. The solution wasn't a new model, it was a new messaging strategy, along with a visual redesign that explained how recommendations were generated. The lesson wasn't just technical; it was psychological and communicative. This is the power of iteration: it widens the aperture of analysis.

Importantly, I also use iteration as a safeguard against overconfidence. A model that performs well today may fail tomorrow if external conditions change. By revisiting models regularly, even ones that seem to be "working", he keeps his systems nimble and his assumptions in check. This is especially crucial in high-stakes contexts like fraud detection or risk scoring, where adversarial behaviors evolve rapidly. Rather than playing catch-up after a breach or misclassification, I build in preemptive change. In his world, waiting until something breaks is not resilience, it is negligence.

At the heart of iteration is a kind of humility. It is the humility to say, "This version is the best we can do now, but not the best we'll ever do." I cultivate this humility not as a weakness but as a strategic strength. It protects against stagnation. It prevents the team from mistaking version 1.0 for a final product. It gives everyone permission to challenge assumptions, update beliefs, and chase better solutions.

In closing, the iteration loop is not a detour rather it is the path. For I, it is the discipline that transforms initial insight into lasting impact. It is what turns a promising prototype into a reliable partner in business decision-making. More than anything, iteration is how resilience gets coded into systems, teams, and strategies. It is not glamorous. It rarely fits into a neat slide deck. But it is the invisible thread that holds innovation together when the first version fails, when the feedback stings, and when the future refuses to stand still. Through iteration, I don't just build models, I build momentum.

CHAPTER 9

L eadership in data science does not begin with command. It begins with clarity. In a landscape where problems are undefined, data is fragmented, and solutions are probabilistic, true leadership is not about giving orders, it's about giving meaning. Leadership is not a role conferred by hierarchy, but a responsibility assumed through vision. It is the ability to illuminate the path forward, rally people across disciplines, and drive innovation not by mandate, but by magnetism.

I have led across varied environments, corporate teams, start-up ecosystems, and cross-border collaborations where I have rarely had formal authority over everyone involved. Instead, it has cultivated influence. Power lies in how you articulate value, how he connects dots that others don't see, and how he translates technical ambitions into organizational relevance. I understand that people don't follow models, they follow momentum, and that momentum is sustained by belief: belief in the mission, in the direction, and in the capacity to reach it together.

At the core of my leadership approach is narrative. You do not begin projects by showcasing code or dashboards. It begins with a story about the customer whose experience could be transformed, the inefficiency that could be eradicated, or the insight waiting to be unlocked. I tell stories not as embellishments but as frameworks for alignment. When team members understand why a project matters, they become more invested in how it unfolds. A well-crafted narrative becomes the connective tissue between disciplines from data scientists, product designers, marketers, operations managers all anchoring to the same vision even as they speak different professional languages.

One of the greatest assets as a leader is his fluency across those languages. He can move fluidly from a technical conversation about neural network regularization to a strategic discussion on quarterly goals to a user-centered dialogue about onboarding friction. This ability to switch registers allows me to serve as an interpreter between domains explaining business constraints to technical teams and technical possibilities to business teams. In doing so, he reduces friction and fosters respect. People follow me because he listens before he leads. He doesn't impose a vision; he co-develops one, ensuring that everyone sees their fingerprints on the outcome.

A vivid example of this occurred during a project aimed at reducing loan default rates in a microfinance network. The data science team was eager to develop a sophisticated risk model using credit scores, transaction data, and behavioral analytics. However, the field agents who actually disbursed and recovered loans were skeptical. They worried that algorithmic scoring would replace their judgment and diminish their relationships with borrowers. Rather than pushing the model through, I convened a series of listening sessions. He invited field agents to describe how they assess trustworthiness, what red flags they look for, and why some borrowers defy data expectations. Then he used those insights to co-design features and establish explainability criteria that gave agents visibility into model logic. By the time the model was launched, it wasn't just *I's* vision, it was theirs too. Adoption was smooth, and outcomes improved. This, for I, is what influence looks like: not winning arguments, but building shared conviction.

Influence also stems from his or her consistency. In complex projects, where uncertainty is high and timelines shift, people crave clarity. I provide that not by pretending to have all the answers, but by maintaining a steady compass. He is transparent about what's known and what's not. He is quick to highlight risks without dramatizing them. He doesn't overpromise; instead, he builds trust through evidence, honesty, and a relentless focus on learning. When a model underperforms, he doesn't hide it, he narrates it, frames it as an opportunity, and invites the team to help reframe the question. This intellectual humility fosters loyalty and long-term credibility. People trust me not just because he's smart, but because he is grounded.

Importantly, vision is rarely confined to a single department or deliverable. He sees data science not as a service function, but as a strategic lever that reshapes how businesses operate, compete, and serve their communities. He asks provocative questions: What if fraud detection wasn't just about catching crime, but about building customer confidence? What if retention strategies weren't driven by churn metrics, but by shared value with the user? What if internal dashboards didn't just inform executives, but empowered frontline teams? In asking these questions, I elevate the purpose of data science and invite broader participation in its potential. His vision stretches beyond the technical and into the transformational.

But vision, no matter how compelling, must meet the practical. It is deeply attentive to execution. He understands that influence without delivery is just charisma. So, he grounds his aspirational thinking in clear roadmaps, agile iterations, and feedback loops. He measures progress not just by completed sprints, but by how well the team stays aligned to the original intent. He encourages teams to pause mid-project and ask: Are we still solving the right problem? Are we still delivering on the promise we made at the outset? These questions keep the vision alive and adaptive.

Another crucial dimension of leadership is inclusion. He makes room for dissent, welcomes opposing views, and often seeks input from junior colleagues who might bring fresh, unfiltered perspectives. He doesn't lead with ego. He leads with clarity and curiosity. He knows that influence is not about being the smartest person in the room, it's about creating a room where smart decisions can emerge. He cultivates a space where others feel empowered to lead as well.

In conclusion, my approach to leadership redefines what it means to be influential in the data-driven era. It is not about domination; it is about direction. It is not about control; it is about coherence. By leading through vision, listening, storytelling, and trust, he mobilizes people across departments, industries, and continents. His leadership leaves behind more than completed projects, it leaves behind alignment, understanding, and belief. In the end, it is not just the systems I build that create change, it is the shared momentum he or she inspires.

Innovation in data science does not happen in isolation. It requires the synthesis of diverse perspectives, each bringing its own assumptions, tools, priorities, and constraints. Business leaders want clarity and speed. Designers value empathy and usability. Engineers seek scalability and system integrity. Legal teams focus on risk, while marketers prioritize customer resonance. And then there are the data scientists, balancing statistical rigor, computational complexity, and real-world messiness. In this mosaic of expertise, progress hinges on one thing: collaboration. For me, leadership means not just having a clear vision but building the bridges necessary to bring that vision to life across boundaries, disciplines, and mindsets.

Cross-disciplinary collaboration is notoriously difficult, not because people are unwilling to cooperate, but because they speak different operational languages. A product manager might talk about "pain points," while a machine learning engineer speaks in "hyperparameters." A compliance officer worries about "regulatory exposure," while a developer thinks in terms of "latency." These aren't just semantic differences, they reflect distinct mental models. The genius lies in his ability to harmonize these models. He doesn't force uniformity; instead, he facilitates translation. His meetings feel less like battlegrounds of opinion and more like cross-cultural exchanges, spaces where each voice is decoded, respected, and integrated.

One of my foundational strategies is pre-collaboration alignment. Before any large-scale initiative begins, he brings all stakeholders into the same room not just to assign tasks, but to align assumptions. In these sessions, I encourage everyone to articulate their priorities, fears, definitions of success, and red lines. He asks foundational questions: What will make this project meaningful to you? What does failure look like? What does your team need to trust this solution? These early moments of honesty prevent late-stage friction. They also foster mutual accountability. When disagreements later arise and they always do, there is a shared foundation to return to.

I also employ a principle he calls "dual comprehension." Every key contributor should understand not only their domain responsibilities but also how their decisions ripple across other teams. He encourages engineers to sit in on customer interviews. He invites marketing leaders to observe data model reviews. He has designers present user journey insights to data scientists so that feature selection is informed by empathy, not just correlation. In one notable project involving the launch of a recommendation system for a content platform, I paired UX designers with model engineers during the feature ideation phase. This collaboration

117

led to the inclusion of subtle but meaningful indicators like content pacing preferences or interaction pauses that had a profound effect on user satisfaction. Neither team could have identified these signals alone. Together, they built something that felt both technically elegant and deeply human.

Conflict, of course, is inevitable in collaborative work. Deadlines clash with data availability. Legal reviews slow technical rollouts. Business urgency pushes against scientific caution. I don't try to eliminate conflict rather harness it. He frames tension as a signal, not a problem. When a compliance lead raises concerns about data privacy, I don't downplay it; he explores how that concern might lead to stronger architecture or better user consent design. When a developer resists a last-minute change from marketing, I step in not to referee, but to reframe: What are we really solving for? What are the long-term costs of this compromise? By facilitating principled negotiation rather than positional standoffs, he turns conflict into clarity.

Another hallmark of cross-disciplinary leadership is his ability to craft collaborative artifacts. These are documents, dashboards, workflows, and visual models that help disparate teams anchor their contributions. For instance, in a fraud detection program that required input from operations, cybersecurity, customer service, and data science, I developed a shared risk taxonomy. This living document defined what different teams meant by "suspicious behavior," "false positive," or "priority escalation." It served as a Rosetta Stone, ensuring that teams did not talk past each other. The artifact didn't just clarify semantics; it created a sense of shared ownership and reduced misunderstanding. For me, the artifact is never a formality; it is a bridge.

Importantly, I am mindful of power dynamics in cross-functional spaces. He knows that technical teams often have more perceived authority in innovation settings. To counteract this, he makes deliberate space for underrepresented voices. In retrospectives, he prompts the quiet contributors to speak first. He defers to domain experts when trade-offs arise in unfamiliar terrain. He credits ideas accurately, especially when they emerge from unexpected quarters. This inclusive approach not only builds trust, it enriches outcomes. Diverse teams don't just perform better because of representation; they perform better because they have more vantage points, more contradictions to resolve, and more constraints to navigate. I don't just manage this complexity, he leverages it.

Cross-disciplinary collaboration also extends to your relationship with leadership. He actively educates senior executives on the limits and potentials of data science, ensuring that expectations remain grounded in reality. He resists the temptation to oversell capabilities, choosing instead to build credibility through transparency and consistent delivery. When leadership asks for metrics that the current data cannot support, I explain why, offer alternative proxies, and recommend responsible paths forward. A leader doesn't defer blindly, nor does he stonewall, he dialogues. In doing so, he earns the respect of those above me and becomes a trusted translator between vision and viability.

At its heart, collaborative practice is a form of respect. It is the belief that no one discipline holds all the answers, and that solutions worthy of deployment must first be worthy of collective effort. He sees collaboration not as a transactional requirement, but as a creative force, one that produces ideas richer than any single brain or background could conjure. His leadership, therefore, is not about being at the center of the room. It is about building the room itself: a space where smart people can disagree productively, build jointly, and celebrate progress together.

In conclusion, leading across disciplines requires more than facilitation, it demands fluency, humility, empathy, and structure. I embody all four. Through preemptive alignment, dual comprehension, constructive conflict, and shared ownership, he transforms the chaos of cross-functional work into a choreography of insight. His bridges are not just organizational, they are intellectual and emotional, forged in trust and curiosity. And with each project that spans boundaries, I reaffirm a simple truth: that innovation, at its best, is a team sport.

In any team tasked with building the future, the greatest threat is not ignorance, it is silence. It is the moment when someone has an objection but stays quiet. When a developer sees a flaw but decides not to raise it. When a junior analyst has an idea but assumes it's not welcome. In high-performance, high-pressure environments, fear can masquerade as professionalism. And where fear takes root, creativity withers. For me, psychological safety is not a soft ideal, it is a strategic imperative. It is the oxygen that allows teams to think boldly, act decisively, and learn quickly. Without it, even the most talented teams underperform. With it, even imperfect systems evolve.

Psychological safety, as I understand it, is not the absence of tension, it is the presence of trust. It is the belief that one can speak up without fear of humiliation or retaliation. That feedback will be heard, not punished. That risk-taking is expected, and failure when it comes is an opportunity, not an indictment. This kind of culture does not emerge by accident. It must be modeled, reinforced, and protected. I do all three, treating psychological safety as a core design feature of every team he leads.

One of the most visible ways I cultivate this safety is through how one handles failure. When a model performs poorly or a strategy falls short, he avoids the language of blame. Instead, he begins postmortems with open-ended questions: *What surprised us? What did we miss? What assumptions did we make that didn't hold?* He frames every failure as a systems issue, not a personal one. Over time, this shifts how the team experiences setbacks. Instead of defensiveness, there is inquiry. Instead of withdrawal, there is engagement. In this world, the phrase "I was wrong" is not an admission of weakness, it's a sign of maturity.

He also pays close attention to team meetings and communication dynamics. In brainstorming sessions, he deliberately holds back from speaking first, allowing others to shape the direction before he weighs in. In technical discussions, he invites questions from non-technical colleagues, signaling that everyone's understanding matters. He watches body language, listens to the unsaid, and checks in privately with quieter team members. If a mistake occurs in execution, It is quick to share responsibility publicly even when the decision was made by others. This practice of shielded accountability encourages risk-taking because it assures the team that their leader will absorb the shock while helping them learn from it.

Another way I foster psychological safety is by democratizing contribution. He actively dismantles hierarchies that inhibit expression. A new hire's comment receives the same attention as a senior engineer's suggestion. He emphasizes role fluidity in problem-solving, encouraging product managers to explore data questions, analysts to offer UX insights, and engineers to voice business concerns. This multidirectional respect prevents silos and creates space for holistic thinking. When people feel seen beyond their job title, they show up more fully and they bring their best ideas with them.

I also understand the emotional labor that comes with innovation. The stress of uncertainty. The fatigue of iteration. The vulnerability of putting unfinished ideas on the table. To support his teams, he introduces rituals of restoration: off-the-record check-ins, anonymous pulse surveys, "win +

learn" sessions that celebrate both accomplishments and near-misses. These rituals are not distractions from productivity; they are enablers of it. They remind people that they are more than resources; they are human beings navigating ambiguity together.

Perhaps the most profound way I model psychological safety is through his own openness. He admits when he doesn't know. He shares his own moments of doubt. He asks for feedback on his leadership style and takes it seriously. This self-awareness flattens hierarchy and shows that authority is compatible with humility. In one instance, a junior data scientist challenged the framing of a problem I had initially proposed. Rather than defending it, I invited her to lead a reframing workshop. The resulting shift improved both model performance and stakeholder alignment. That act of empowerment sent a message far beyond that project: it said, "Your voice matters, and your perspective is powerful."

I also train other leaders within his team to cultivate safety. He mentors managers on how to give feedback that uplifts rather than shames, how to intervene when someone is being silenced, and how to handle conflict with compassion. He shares stories from his own leadership journey, not just successes, but mistakes that taught me empathy. In doing so, he creates a ripple effect where safety becomes not just a team value but an organizational muscle.

Importantly, I view psychological safety not just as a benefit to team morale, but as a performance multiplier. Safe teams iterate faster because they waste less energy on politics and fear. They innovate more boldly because they are not punished for taking smart risks. They attract and retain better talent because people want to work where they are trusted. They resolve conflicts more cleanly, because feedback is a norm, not a rupture. In short, they are not just happier, they are more effective.

There is a final, often overlooked, dimension to my commitment to psychological safety: justice. He knows that safety is unevenly distributed. That people from marginalized backgrounds often carry the burden of extra vigilance, extra code-switching, extra self-editing. I work to counter this not with tokenism, but with systems. He creates onboarding processes that demystify culture. He sets ground rules in meetings that protect against interruption and appropriation. He calls out unconscious bias and invites ongoing education. He believes that a truly safe environment is one where the quietest voice does not have to shout to be heard.

Psychological safety is not a leadership style; it is a strategic foundation. It is the condition under which creativity, collaboration, and courage become possible. I build this foundation deliberately and defend it fiercely. He knows that in a field as complex and fast-moving as data science, the edge does not come from more tools or smarter algorithms, it comes from better human dynamics. And at the center of those dynamics is trust: the trust to speak, to challenge, to grow, and to belong. In fostering that trust, I ensure that teams are not only productive, but fearless.

CHAPTER 10

As the scale, speed, and sophistication of intelligent systems grow, so too does the need for architectures that respect the boundaries of privacy, latency, and sovereignty. In the early days of data science, centralization was king, data was pooled into vast warehouses, processed by monolithic models, and served back to end-users from centralized clouds. But today, this paradigm is being reimagined. Not because it failed, but because it cannot meet the ethical, technical, and social expectations of the next frontier. This shift is not just a trend; it is a reckoning. A necessary pivot toward systems that are smarter, closer, and fairer. He sees the future not as more centralized intelligence, but more distributed wisdom.

One of the most transformative concepts I have embraced is federated learning, which is a model training technique where data stays local and only insights are aggregated centrally. In this architecture, personal devices like smartphones or edge sensors contribute to the training of a global model without ever sharing raw data. For me, this represents a seismic shift in how we think about ownership and agency. Instead of forcing users to surrender their data to improve an algorithm, federated learning reverses the flow: the model comes to the data. This not only enhances privacy, it democratizes participation in AI.

I first explored federated learning in a healthcare setting, where multiple hospitals wanted to collaborate on predictive models for early diagnosis but were legally and ethically barred from sharing patient records. Traditional machine learning approaches demanded data centralization, an impossible task in this context. But by implementing federated learning, I enabled each institution to train locally on their own data and contribute model gradients to a shared, evolving model. The result was a breakthrough: improved diagnostic accuracy without compromising privacy. It was also a revelation. The model didn't just work; it respected the context in which it operated.

But federated learning is only one piece of the puzzle. For truly responsive, real-time intelligence, I turned his focus to edge AI, the deployment of models directly on devices like wearables, industrial sensors, or autonomous drones. These systems require low-latency decision-making in environments where sending data to the cloud would be too slow, too expensive, or too risky. Edge AI is not about shrinking models; it's about rethinking them. Its work in logistics, for example, involved optimizing delivery routes based on traffic, fuel cost, and temperature conditions, all of which changed minute by minute. By deploying lightweight models on vehicle-mounted IoT devices, decisions could be made on the spot, with no need for centralized coordination. The edge became not just a receiver of decisions, but a generator of them.

The implications are vast. In smart cities, edge AI enables faster responses to environmental or security anomalies. In manufacturing, it supports predictive maintenance without interrupting production lines. In financial services, it allows fraud detection algorithms to run in real time on customer devices, reducing reaction time from seconds to milliseconds. The power of the edge lies in its intimacy; it understands context in ways the cloud never could. It lives in the moment, at the point of action.

Yet, decentralization introduces new design challenges. Synchronization, security, and governance become more complex when intelligence is distributed. I have responded by advocating for decentralized intelligence frameworks that blend technical resilience with ethical foresight. These systems are built not just to function at the margins, but to learn from them. They adapt locally, report globally, and update collaboratively. I often describe them as "constellations of intelligence", interconnected nodes that share learning without surrendering autonomy.

A striking example of this thinking came during his work on a cross-border agricultural intelligence platform. Farmers in different regions contributed crop data, soil conditions, and yield metrics. The challenge was to create a recommendation engine that respected regional variation while still learning globally. A centralized model would have averaged out the nuance. But by designing a multi-tiered system, local models that adapted to microclimates, with periodic sharing of key learnings to a central layer, I enabled both specificity and scalability. Each node in the network grew smarter, and the collective did too. It was decentralization as strength, not compromise.

This architectural future also aligns with my ethical framework. He has long been skeptical of data practices that treat users as extractable resources. In centralized systems, the burden of trust falls disproportionately on the individual trusting that their data won't be misused, sold, or breached. In decentralized systems, trust is embedded in the design. Data does not need to move. Consent is not buried in terms of service; it is intrinsic to the protocol. I see this not just as good engineering, but as moral progress. A system that protects people by default is a system worth building.

Still, I am clear-eyed about the trade-offs. Federated learning requires robust coordination infrastructure, secure aggregation methods, and defenses against model inversion attacks. Edge AI demands power-efficient algorithms and model compression techniques that preserve accuracy without overfitting. Decentralized intelligence can introduce fragmentation and inconsistency if not carefully orchestrated. But these are not insurmountable obstacles. They are design tensions, signals of a system maturing. I don't view them as reasons to retreat, but as prompts to innovate smarter.

I also understand that architecture is destiny. The choices we make about where and how intelligence lives will shape who benefits from it. Centralized systems concentrate power. Decentralized systems distribute it. The former may optimize for efficiency; the latter, for resilience. I believe the future requires both but with a decisive shift toward models that empower individuals, protect context, and scale through federation, not domination.

As emerging technologies like 6G, quantum computing, and on-device LLMs come into view, I remain focused on the foundational question: What kind of intelligence do we want to build, and who gets to shape it? For me, the answer lies not in technical supremacy, but in architectural humility, systems designed to serve, to adapt, and to respect. The future will not be won by bigger models or faster GPUs alone. It will be defined by where intelligence resides, how it travels, and who remains in control of their story.

As machine learning systems grow in capability, they often grow in opacity. Deep neural networks can detect fraud, generate images, and translate languages but they cannot always explain why. They are powerful, but they are not transparent. This is not merely a technical concern; it is a societal one. When systems that influence loans, healthcare, security, or legal decisions become black boxes, trust is eroded, and accountability becomes elusive. In a world increasingly shaped by intelligent infrastructure, I argue that clarity is not a luxury, it is a requirement. Explainability is no longer optional. It is the currency of responsible AI.

The promise of artificial intelligence was never just automation. It was an augmentation. The idea that machines could extend human judgment does not replace it. But augmentation requires understanding. A doctor won't act on a diagnosis suggested by an algorithm unless she understands its basis. A judge won't rely on a recidivism score if the rationale is hidden behind layers of abstraction. An operations lead won't greenlight an anomaly alert if it can't be traced to input factors. I believe that when AI cannot be explained, it cannot be trusted and when it cannot be trusted, it cannot scale.

To address this, I have championed the integration of explainable AI (XAI) methods at every stage of model development. But he is quick to note that explainability is not a single tool or technique, it is a mindset. It begins before the first line of code. In framing the problem: Is it appropriate for a model to make this decision? In selecting features: Are we including variables that reflect bias, correlation without causation, or proxies for protected attributes? And in evaluating results: Are we prioritizing interpretability alongside accuracy? For I, explainability is not a constraint, it is a design principle.

In my work with financial institutions, I have faced real pressure to balance performance with transparency. Credit scoring models, for instance, must be not only predictive but also defensible to regulators and fair to applicants. A purely black box model no matter how accurate would be rejected outright. I addressed this by leveraging tools like SHAP (SHapley Additive exPlanations) to break down model predictions into contributions from individual features. With SHAP, stakeholders could see precisely how much a missed repayment, a short credit history, or a high utilization ratio affected a score. This allowed underwriters to review decisions with confidence and gave applicants a clear, factual explanation for outcomes. The model didn't just predict, it communicated.

Beyond SHAP, I use methods like LIME (Local Interpretable Model-Agnostic Explanations) to create surrogate models that approximate black-box behavior in a localized, human-readable form. This is especially useful in systems where different users interact with the model in different ways. A global explanation might satisfy a compliance officer, but a localized one might be what a customer service agent needs to answer a complaint. I have also adopted counterfactual analysis, where models answer the question: *What would need to change for this outcome to be different?* This not only empowers users but reveals the boundaries of the model's reasoning.

However, I am careful not to conflate explainability with simplification. Some decisions are inherently complex, and not every stakeholder needs to see the same level of detail. The goal is not to make every model intuitive to a layperson, it is to make every model accountable. That means building systems where explanations are contextual, layered, and audience specific. Executives might need a dashboard summary. Engineers need code-level traceability. Regulators need documentation. End-users need fairness and recourse. I design explainability frameworks that serve each of these needs simultaneously, often embedding them into the product interface itself.

I also advocate for a shift in how success is measured. Traditional machine learning optimization focuses on metrics like accuracy, precision, or AUC. But an opaque model with 90% accuracy may be less valuable than a transparent one with 85% especially in high-stakes domains. He encourages teams to expand their definition of performance to include trustworthiness, legibility, and fairness. In internal reviews, he poses questions like: Would we feel comfortable explaining this model to a skeptical journalist? Could a user appeal this decision with evidence? Would the same features be chosen if the model were trained in a different population? These questions elevate explainability from a box-ticking exercise to an ethical commitment.

Importantly, I see explainable AI as not just a technical challenge, but a cultural one. Too often, teams get attached to the elegance of their models and bristle at questions that imply limitation. I counter this by creating an environment where challenge is encouraged. He normalizes uncertainty. He praises those who surface ambiguity. He embeds "explainability reviews" alongside code reviews and encourages interdisciplinary feedback. In one memorable project, a product manager questioned why a high-performing churn model recommended downgrading a segment of loyal users. Upon closer inspection, the model had learned that those users rarely called customer service, a proxy it interpreted as disengagement. The team revised the training data, updated the feature definitions, and avoided a decision that would have backfired. Without a culture of explainability, this insight would have been lost.

The need for explainability is especially urgent in emerging contexts like generative AI, autonomous systems, and real-time decision engines. As models begin to generate content, initiate actions, or respond dynamically to the world, the potential for harm increases. I argue that explainability must evolve in parallel not just explaining what a system did, but why it believed that was appropriate. This involves a new class of tools: attention maps, decision trees layered on embeddings, dialogue tracing, and more. It also involves human-machine interaction design ensuring that explanations are intelligible, timely, and useful.

This isn't just about mitigating risk. It's about deepening engagement. When users understand how systems make decisions, they trust them more. They use them more intelligently. They give more accurate feedback.

Explainability creates a loop of learning not just for machines, but for organizations. It enables systems to grow not just in performance, but in relevance.

In conclusion, as the complexity of AI systems grows, so must our capacity to understand them. Trust in the machine age will not be earned by accuracy alone; it will be earned by clarity. My approach to explainability is holistic, rigorous, and human-centered. He doesn't seek to make AI simpler than it is, it seeks to make it as transparent as it *needs* to be. In doing so, he builds systems not just of intelligence, but of integrity. And in a world flooded with opaque predictions, he lights the path with explanation.

The future of intelligent infrastructure will not be shaped solely by engineers or algorithms, but by the people who steward them. As artificial intelligence becomes woven into the fabric of everyday life from public health to finance, governance to education the question is no longer just how powerful these systems can be, but how responsibly they can be built and sustained. Leadership in this new era demands more than technical expertise. It requires foresight, humility, and a moral compass that points beyond the product roadmap. It demands a new generation of data stewards prepared not only to solve problems, but to question which problems are worth solving.

The foundations of this kind of leadership begin with intellectual discipline. A strong data leader must be both expansive and precise, capable of exploring ideas from multiple disciplines while remaining rigorous in analysis. It is no longer enough to know how to code a model or tune a hyperparameter. Leaders must understand the policy environment in which their systems operate, the social context their tools affect, and the historical patterns that shape data. Mathematics and ethics must coexist in the same decision loop. Curiosity becomes a survival trait, and complexity is not something to eliminate, but to embrace responsibly.

Among the most important qualities in tomorrow's data stewards is critical reflection. Not every insight should be deployed. Not every dataset should be used. The presence of data does not imply its neutrality, nor does the success of a model imply its legitimacy. Decisions must be guided by questions that extend beyond feasibility: Who benefits from this system? Who is excluded? What assumptions are embedded in the architecture? These are not afterthoughts, they are prerequisites. A leader who cannot pause to interrogate their own work risks automating harm at scale.

Equally essential is the ability to navigate trade-offs. Building intelligent systems often involves competing values: speed versus accuracy, innovation versus regulation, personalization versus privacy. Rarely is the optimal path clear-cut. The most effective leaders are those who can hold ambiguity without paralysis, communicate trade-offs transparently, and bring multidisciplinary voices into the decision-making process. They don't pretend that every conflict has a perfect solution. Instead, they work to make each solution justifiable, proportionate, and revisable in light of new evidence.

Mentorship and community-building must also be central to this new model of leadership. Knowledge in this field evolves rapidly. No one arrives fully prepared. That's why the cultivation of shared learning environments matters. Future-ready leaders invest in people as much as they invest in products. They create spaces where junior professionals can contribute early, ask questions freely, and see themselves not as support staff, but as core thinkers. They build psychological safety into the team's DNA, understanding that courageous dialogue breeds better outcomes than polite conformity. In this way, leadership becomes less about control and more about catalyzing others' potential.

Communication, often under-emphasized in technical training, is another cornerstone. The ability to translate complexity into clarity whether to executives, regulators, or end-users sets apart those who influence from those who simply build. But this translation is not just linguistic; it is strategic. It means understanding what each audience values and how to speak to those values without diluting the truth. A good leader does not merely simplify, they illuminate. They help others understand both what a system does and what it means.

A long-term leader in AI must also be a custodian of integrity. As intelligent infrastructure begins to define the contours of work, mobility, security, and opportunity, ethical erosion cannot be treated as a manageable risk, it must be averted from the start. This requires embedding principles of fairness, transparency, accountability, and sustainability directly into development processes. It also means building systems that allow for recourse, not just performance. Users should not only experience automation, but they should also be able to question and challenge it. The architecture of inclusion must be active, not reactive.

Preparing for this future also means confronting the myth of neutrality. Data is not a mirror; it is a lens. It reflects the systems that generated it, often embedding disparities in wealth, access, and representation. Leaders cannot afford to be passive recipients of these patterns. They must intervene by correcting bias where it appears, by advocating for more inclusive data collection, and by refusing to deploy systems that entrench injustice under the guise of optimization. The ability to "move fast and fix things" may become the defining skill of the next era.

Sustainability, too, enters the leadership conversation not only in the environmental sense, though carbon impact and energy efficiency must be measured and mitigated but in terms of societal continuity. Can a system adapt to shifting norms and laws? Can its benefits be distributed without concentrating harm? Can it survive the departure of its original architects? Responsible leaders design not only for functionality, but for longevity. They leave behind documentation, community capacity, and institutional memory. In short, they build ecosystems, not just products.

One cannot ignore the importance of courage. Leading in this space will increasingly mean pushing back against commercial pressures, against regulatory shortcuts, against the temptation to prioritize efficiency over ethics. Courage is required to say "no" to lucrative but risky projects, to call out flawed assumptions, or to delay a launch in favor of a more inclusive approach. This is not the courage of grand defiance, but the daily courage of principled decision-making.

At its core, data leadership in the age of intelligent systems is not about being the smartest person in the room. It is about being the person who makes it possible for others to think deeply, act ethically, and innovate responsibly. It is a form of stewardship, not showmanship. It is about asking better questions, cultivating better environments, and building better futures not just for the privileged few who design the systems, but for everyone whose lives they touch.

There will be no shortage of technological advancement in the years to come. But whether that advancement improves lives or amplifies inequities will depend on who is at the helm and how prepared they are to lead with discipline, empathy, and vision. The next generation of data stewards must be trained not only in algorithms, but in accountability. Not only in systems, but in solidarity. They must be prepared to look beyond what is possible and toward what is just. And when they do, they won't just shape the future of AI, they will shape the future of trust itself.

Mentorship is often perceived as an auxiliary function, an optional act of generosity, a goodwill gesture offered by seasoned professionals to their less experienced peers. But in high-impact, high-velocity domains like data science, mentorship is not optional, and it is not peripheral. It is a central methodology, an intentional, structured, and iterative process of knowledge transfer, cultural scaffolding, and leadership cultivation. In environments where technology changes rapidly and ethical stakes remain high; mentorship becomes both a stabilizing force and a catalyst for innovation. It is a mode of thinking, a vehicle for values, and a method for sustaining organizational intelligence over time.

To understand mentorship as methodology, one must begin by reframing what it is and what it is not. It is not the passive exchange of tips from expert to novice. It is not confined to career advice or soft-skill development. It is not a hierarchical lecture delivered at coffee tables or quarterly check-ins. Rather, mentorship is a strategic infrastructure for intellectual continuity and adaptive learning. It functions as a living curriculum embedded within the workplace, an ever-evolving interface between experience and emergence, between what has been mastered and what is yet to be discovered.

The foundation of mentorship-as-methodology lies in its deliberate architecture. Effective mentorship programs are not incidental, they are designed. They are shaped by intentional pairings, mutual accountability, goal-setting rituals, and structured reflection. The design must account for asymmetry in knowledge while creating symmetry in respect. The mentor is not an oracle but a steward. The mentee is not a passive vessel but a co-creator of meaning. In this design, both parties are learners. Both adapt. Both teach.

In data-driven domains, this kind of dynamic is especially critical. The knowledge of half-life is short. Languages, libraries, tools, and protocols evolve at a pace that formal education alone cannot match. Mentorship becomes the bridge between academic abstraction and operational reality. A textbook may explain supervised learning, but it cannot teach how to manage a cross-functional data sprint under real-time pressure. A research paper may describe model fairness metrics, but it does not prepare one to defend those metrics in front of non-technical stakeholders. These nuances live in the experience of practitioners and mentorship becomes the conduit through which that experience is transmitted.

But transmission is not the only value. Mentorship also cultivates interpretive judgment, which cannot be taught directly. Judgment knowing when to break a rule, when to delay a launch, when to take a risk or step back is often the dividing line between technical competence and true leadership. By watching someone navigate uncertainty with integrity, a mentee learns not only what to do, but how to think. This exposure accelerates maturity far more than tutorials or certifications ever could.

At its most impact, mentorship fosters what sociologists call situated learning, which is learning that occurs within context, through participation in a community of practice. In such settings, knowledge is not abstract but embodied. It is embedded in stories, decisions, hesitations, and recoveries. When a mentor explains not just what choice was made but why other choices were rejected, the mentee begins to see complexity not as noise, but as signal. They begin to perceive decisions not as linear outputs, but as moral, strategic, and relational acts.

In this way, mentorship becomes a mechanism for transmitting institutional memory. In fast-growing companies or research groups, it is easy for institutional knowledge to fracture. When senior team members leave, they often take undocumented wisdom with them, context behind design decisions, trade-offs made during tight deadlines, ethical debates that shaped protocols. Without mentorship, this loss is invisible but significant. With mentorship, that memory is transferred through dialogue and demonstration. It is preserved not on a wiki page, but in a mentee's intuition.

Mentorship also acts as a cultural multiplier. Every organization has stated values, but its true culture is reflected in who is promoted, what behavior is rewarded, and how people are developed. Mentorship reinforces or reshapes culture through repetition and modeling. A mentor who prioritizes explainability in machine learning will naturally elevate that value in the mentee. A mentor who interrogates data sources for bias encourages others to do the same. Over time, this shaping of norms becomes self-reinforcing. Culture is not just taught, it is caught.

This cultural transmission is especially powerful in global or cross-functional teams. In such settings, team members often arrive with different assumptions about communication, authority, accountability, and success. Formal onboarding can clarify processes, but only mentorship can surface deeper expectations. For example, a junior engineer may learn from a mentor not just how to file a pull request, but how to advocate for a model choice in a way that respects both technical rigor and product strategy. These subtleties are rarely written down, but they matter enormously. Mentorship reduces friction not by standardizing thought, but by building shared understanding.

In environments concerned with ethics and inclusion, mentorship becomes even more critical. It is well documented that underrepresented individuals in data science and AI fields often face additional barriers not just in access to roles, but in access to informal networks and unspoken knowledge. Mentorship disrupts this exclusion by creating deliberate channels of visibility and advocacy. A mentor can demystify a promotion process, challenge biased feedback, or open doors to opportunities that might otherwise remain closed. More importantly, they can validate the mentee's place in a space that may have been coded against them.

To be clear, mentorship is not a cure-all for structural inequity. But it is a lever, one that shifts the balance slightly, giving those with less institutional capital a chance to accelerate, stabilize, and lead. In this light, mentorship becomes a political act. It is an affirmation of capacity, a redistribution of privilege, and a commitment to institutional change not through policy alone, but through people.

It is also a feedback mechanism for mentors themselves. Those who teach often learn their own discipline more deeply. In explaining a process or principle, mentors uncover their own blind spots. They are reminded of foundational principles they may have internalized but no longer question. They are challenged to evolve. Mentorship thus keeps senior talent fresh not only through exposure to emerging thinkers, but through the discipline of articulation. The ability to explain one's work is not separate from mastery, it is evidence of it.

When designed with care, mentorship can extend beyond the one-to-one model. Peer mentorship, group mentorship, and reverse mentorship can all contribute to a more robust learning ecosystem. Peer mentorship, for instance, allows individuals at similar stages to exchange insight, validate experience, and reduce isolation. Group mentorship creates a forum for multiple voices, enriching the learning process through diversity. Reverse mentorship allows junior professionals to educate more senior colleagues on emerging tools, cultural shifts, or blind spots flipping hierarchy in productive ways. In each case, mentorship becomes less about role and more about dialogue.

Organizations that treat mentorship as methodology do not relegate it to "extra credit" or optional goodwill. They embed it into workflows. They allocate time, track outcomes, and offer support. They reward not just output, but development. They do not ask whether someone is a mentor, they ask how they mentor. Metrics may include retention, skill acceleration, or internal mobility. But beyond metrics, the return on mentorship is resilience. Teams with strong mentorship cultures recover faster, adapt more gracefully, and scale with greater cohesion.

Even as automation expands, the demand for mentorship will grow. Intelligent systems cannot yet teach empathy, coach through doubt, or model ethical reasoning in messy, human contexts. These are human acts. And they are more critical than ever. The proliferation of powerful tools means that the cost of a poor decision scale dramatically. Mentorship slows the decision process just enough to insert reflection. It adds drag to dangerous momentum. It inserts human intelligence into artificial intelligence.

Perhaps most importantly, mentorship humanizes the work. It reminds practitioners that behind every model is a person, and behind every decision is a community. In fields obsessed with scale, mentorship insists on intimacy. In cultures driven by novelty, it insists on continuity. It honors the learner and the lineage. It is, at its best, a refusal to let knowledge become disconnected from care.

In conclusion, mentorship is not a side activity in technical work, it is an essential practice. It is both method and message, both structure and spirit. It builds capability, conveys values, mitigates risk, and fosters leadership. As a methodology, it can be scaled, adapted, evaluated, and improved. As a philosophy, it can infuse organizations with coherence and conscience. In a field defined by rapid change, mentorship offers something rare: continuity with meaning. The next era of innovation will not be led by knowledge alone, but by relationships that sustain it. Mentorship is how those relationships begin and how intelligent systems remain, ultimately, human.

REVIEW

"This book is a masterclass in technical depth, ethical reflection, and strategic clarity. Tosin's journey through the landscape of intelligent infrastructure is both compelling and instructive, bridging data science with humanity, precision with empathy, and innovation with responsibility. A vital read for anyone building or navigating the future of intelligent systems."

Dr. Kelechi A., Professor of Artificial Intelligence and Ethics

"A powerful synthesis of technical excellence and moral clarity. This work redefines what it means to be a data scientist in an age of intelligent infrastructure. Every chapter balances depth with accessibility, foresight with humility."

Dr. Amaka Izu, Chair of Computational Social Systems, Tech Solutions Organizations

"This book doesn't just showcase expertise, it builds trust. It's rare to find such a seamless blend of storytelling, engineering rigor, and ethical responsibility in a single volume."

James Halvorson, CTO, Veritas Systems

"A must-read for any leader navigating the intersection of AI and society. It challenges assumptions, provokes critical thought, and offers actionable insight. It's not just a contribution to literature; it's a contribution to leadership."

Lola Anene, Director of Digital Strategy, Open Governance Africa

"From anomaly detection to decentralized intelligence, this work is both a field guide and a philosophical meditation. It charts a clear path for building systems that are as ethical as they are intelligent."

Dr. Leon Richter, Lead Scientist, Data Ethics Institute, Berlin

"Every page affirms the central truth: that data science is not just about numbers, but about people. This is one of the most thoughtful and forward-looking texts I've encountered in the discipline."

Chioma Nwoke, Senior Product Manager, Synapse Analytics

"This is not just a book about building models. It's about building cultures of safety, clarity, and integrity. It should be required reading for every data team.

"Farouk El-Mansour, VP of Engineering, Net Core AI

"Rarely does a book speak so well to both the engineer and the executive. It's deeply technical yet profoundly human, a blueprint for sustainable innovation in complex environments.

" Ngozi Akande, Policy Fellow, Center for Responsible Technology